Ages 5-6

Key Stage 1

Gold Stars®

Supports the National Curriculum Key Stage 1

Bumper Workbook

Ready for School

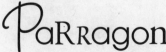

PaRragon

Bath · New York · Singapore · Hong Kong · Cologne · Delhi
Melbourne · Amsterdam · Johannesburg · Auckland · Shenzhen

Written by Betty Root, Monica Hughes, Peter Patilla and Paul Broadbent
Educational Consultants: Stephanie Cooper and Christine Vaughan
Illustrated by Adam Linley
Cover illustrated by Simon Abbot

This edition published by Parragon in 2012

Parragon
Queen Street House
4 Queen Street
BATH, BA1 1HE, UK
www.parragon.com

ISBN 978-1-4454-7833-3

Printed in China

Contents

English

Helping your child

⭐ The activities in this book will help your child to learn about English. Pictures provide hints and clues to support their reading.

⭐ Your child will gain the confidence to: read and write independently, use comprehension skills effectively, look for clues to answer questions and follow instructions.

⭐ Your child will learn about: labels, days of the week, alphabetical order, capital letters and full stops, sequencing, stories and word banks.

⭐ Set aside time to do the activities together. Do a little at a time so that your child enjoys learning.

⭐ Give lots of encouragement and praise. Use the gold stars as rewards and incentives.

⭐ The answers are on page 124.

Contents

All about me

Write in the missing words.

My name is _____.

I am _____ years old.

I live at _____

_____

_____.

My school is called _____.

 My favourite animal is _____.

My favourite sport is _____.

Draw yourself in the box.
Read the words and draw a line to the right part.

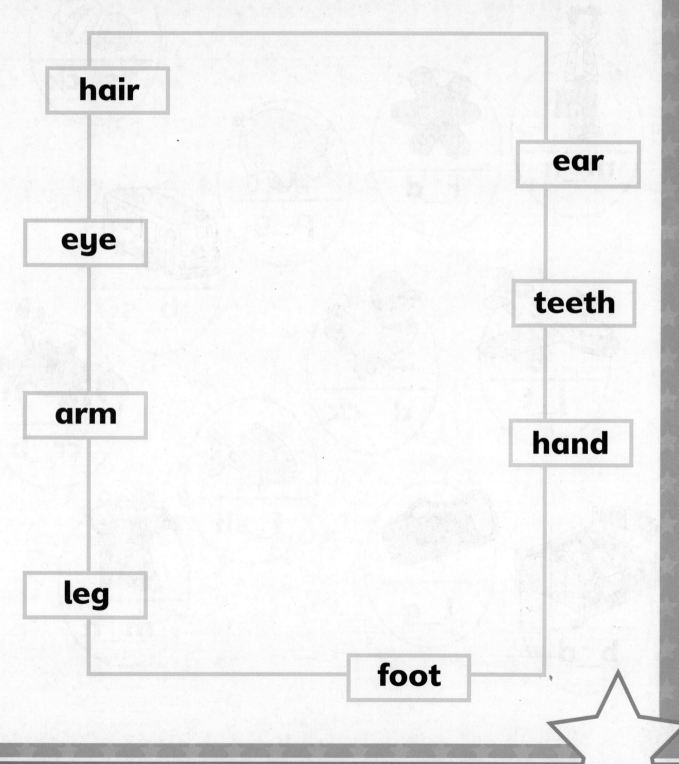

hair

ear

eye

teeth

arm

hand

leg

foot

Note for parent: Labelling helps your child to associate objects with their words and is an important English skill for this age group.

Middle vowel sounds

Use the vowels **a, e, i, o** or **u** to complete the words below.

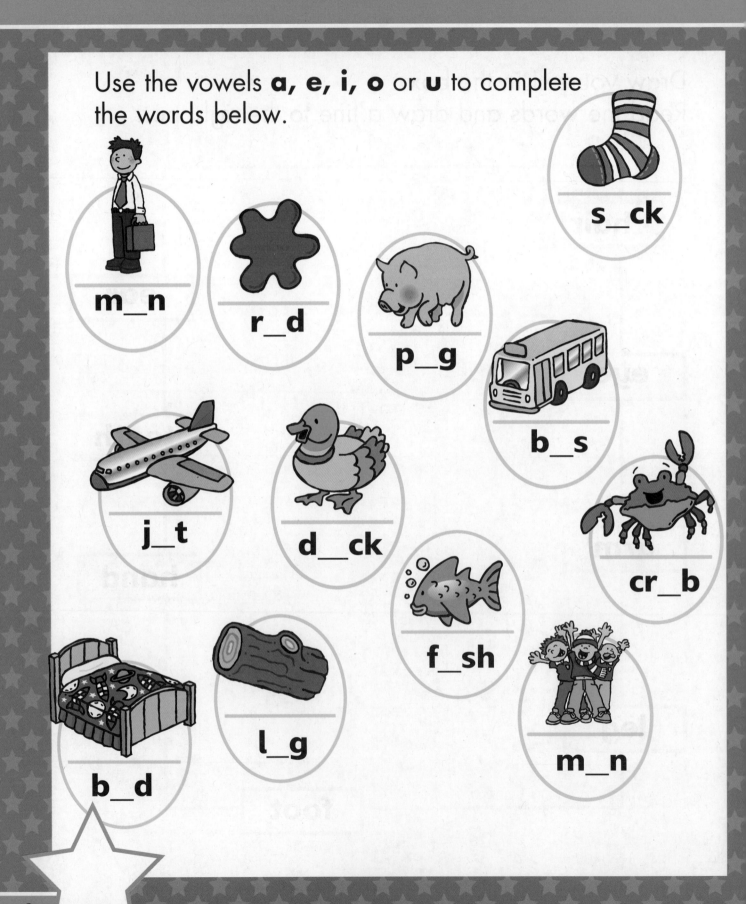

m_ _n

r_d

p_g

s_ _ck

j_t

d_ _ck

b_ _s

cr_ _b

f_sh

b_d

l_g

m_ _n

Join the pictures that have the same middle sounds – **a, e, i, o** or **u**.

Note for parent: These activities give your child experience in identifying vowel sounds in words.

9

Odd one out

Cross out the picture in each row that does not belong.

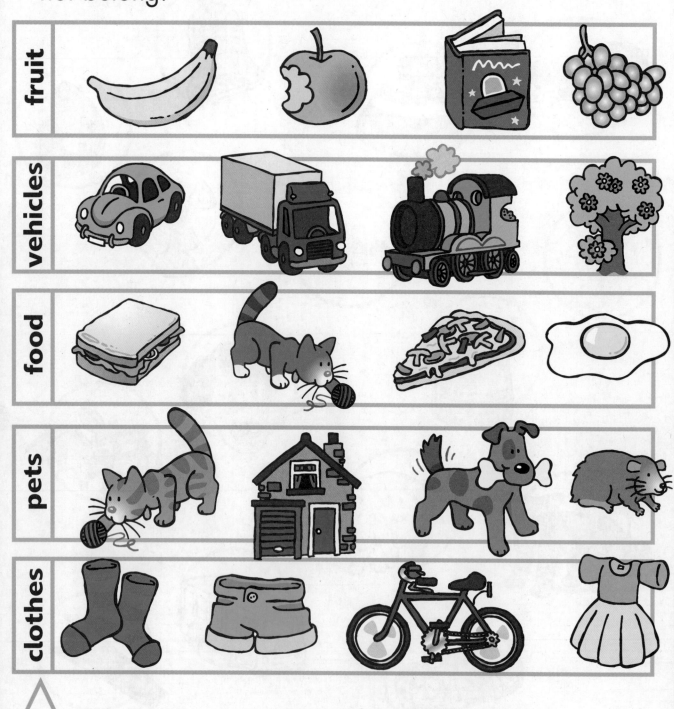

fruit

vehicles

food

pets

clothes

Note for parent: This activity helps your child to classify objects.

Yes or no?

Look at the picture. Read the sentences and write **yes** or **no** next to each one.

The teacher is under the table.   _____

The girl is reading a book.   _____

The boy is painting the door.   _____

The teacher is looking at the girl.   _____

The cat is reading a book.   _____

The boy has got a brush.   _____

The hamster is on its cage.   _____

Note for parent: This activity helps your child begin to understand simple comprehension, looking for picture and word clues to help them find their answers.

11

Writing labels

Read these words:

ball   boy   girl   man   car   tree

Now choose a word to write in each box, to label the picture.

Note for parent: This activity gives practice with reading words and placing them in the correct context.

The alphabet

Write in the missing letters. Some are capital letters and some are lower-case ones.
Draw your own pictures in the empty squares.

Note for parent: This activity helps with capital letters and beginning sounds.

13

Look at these pictures and say each beginning sound.

bl   **br**   **cl**   **cr**

Fill in the missing letters.

_ _ock   _ _idge   _ _own   _ _ack

Now do the same again.

dr   **fl**   **gr**   **pl**

_ _een   _ _ug   _ _ill   _ _ag

Look at the first picture in each row.
Tick the other pictures in the same row that start in the same way.

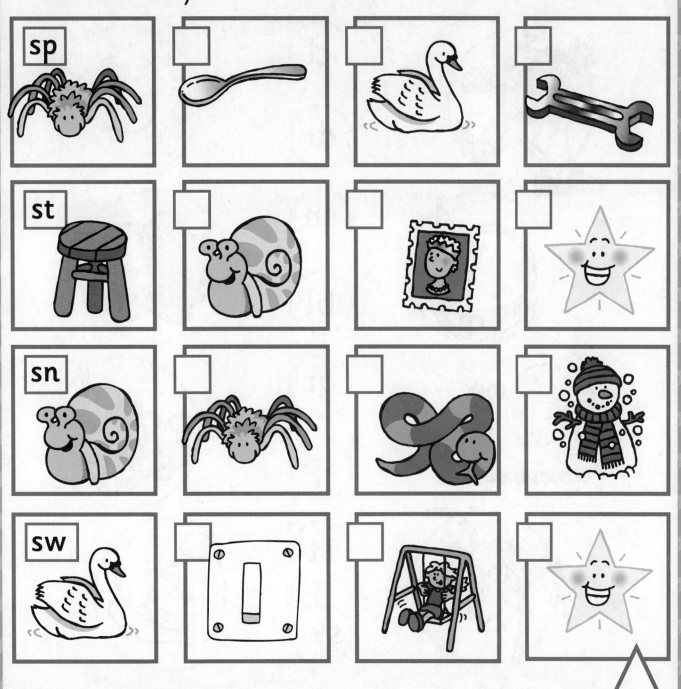

Note for parent: This activity helps your child to identify and use 12 consonant blends at the beginning of words.

15

Quick quiz

Join each sound to a picture. Say the picture names out loud to help you.

cl

dr

sn

bl

gr

sp

st

sw

Note for parent: This is a chance to revise consonant sounds.

Read and draw

Read the sentences and finish the picture.

Draw a tree <u>by</u> the river.
Draw a boat going <u>under</u> the bridge.
Draw a duck <u>on</u> the river.
Draw a car going <u>over</u> the bridge.
Draw a sun <u>up</u> in the sky.

The Enormous Turnip

Look at the pictures. Read the sentences.
Match each sentence to the correct picture.

Everyone fell over and the turnip came out. __

The farmer saw an enormous turnip. __

Everyone tried to pull up the turnip. __

The farmer tried to pull up the turnip. __

Note for parent: This activity gives your child practice in sequencing and making sense of a simple story.

How does it end?

Look at each row of pictures. Tell the story but choose the ending that you like the best.

Note for parent: This activity gives your child experience of telling a simple story in their own words, making sense of pictures and placing events in a logical order.

19

a b c d e f g h i j k l m n o p q r s t u v w x y z

Write the beginning sound of each picture.
Then put the three letters in each row in
alphabetical order.

Note for parent: Two skills are required for this activity: knowing
beginning sounds and alphabetical order.

Little words

Find each little word in one of the big words and then join them with a line.

or

us

an

all

am

in

at

lamb

fork

twins

bat

man

ball

bus

How many of the little words can you read? _____

Find the right word

| sun   bed   boy   ball   girl   tree |

Choose one of these words to write in each sentence.

A little __girl__ put on her dress.

The _____ was hot.

I like getting into my _____ to go to sleep.

I can see a bird's nest in the _____ .

Dad kicked the _____ .

A little _____ put on his football boots.

Note for parent: This activity gives your child the opportunity to complete simple sentences using familiar words. Ask them to read each sentence and point out the capital letters and full stops.

Making sentences

These sentences are all muddled. Write them in the right order and then finish each one with a full stop . or a question mark ?

is time What the

_____

fruit I to like eat

_____

do go school When I to

_____

car going The was fast

_____

up Who the with went Jill hill

_____

on lap The likes sit to my cat

_____

How many capital letters can you count?____

Note for parent: This activity gives further practice with sentences, using capital letters and punctuation.

23

Alphabetical order

Look at the names and then write them in the register in the correct order. Remember to use capital letters.

Note for parent: This activity helps children to practise using alphabetical order for a familiar situation.

Days of the week

Look at the pictures. Read the questions and then write the correct day. Remember the capital letters.

Clare

Jack

Monday

Tuesday

Wednesday

Thursday

When does Clare go trampolining? _____

When does Clare watch television? _____

When does Jack go to the library? _____

When does Clare go shopping? _____

When does Jack wash the car? _____

When does Clare take the dog out? _____

When does Jack play football? _____

Friday

Saturday

Sunday

Note for parent: This activity helps your child to use their comprehension skills as well as learn to write the days of the week.

25

Find your way

Read these instructions. Draw the correct way from the house to the school.

Start at **✗**.

Walk down the path and turn out of the gate.

Turn right after the trees.

Walk along the path to the traffic lights.

Go over the zebra crossing.

Turn right and then turn left into **School Road**.

Go past the fence and turn left through the school gate.

Note for parent: This activity helps your child to understand and follow instructions.

Telephone numbers

Use this telephone directory to answer the questions at the bottom of the page.

Mr Anderson	9802	*Mr Mead*	9980
Mr Caswell	9146	*Miss Palmer*	9544
Mrs Depster	9829	*Mr Shah*	9827
Miss Heelan	9026	*Mrs Todd*	9412
Ms Kamara	9530	*Ms Walker*	9361

What is Mr Shah's number? _____

What is Miss Heelan's number? _____

What is Mr Caswell's number? _____

What is Miss Palmer's number? _____

Whose number is 9361? _____

Whose number is 9802? _____

Whose number is 9412? _____

Whose number is 9829? _____

Do you know your own
telephone number at home? _____

Note for parent: This activity lets your child read for information.

27

Animal dictionary

Match each word to the correct meaning.
Draw a line to join them.

elephant

A large animal that can jump very well. It carries its young in a pouch. It comes from Australia.

kangaroo

A small animal with long arms and feet that it uses like hands. It lives in jungles.

monkey

A large animal with a long trunk and ivory tusks. It lives in Africa and Asia.

panda

An animal like a horse with black and white stripes. It lives in Africa.

zebra

A black and white animal like a bear. It lives in China.

Note for parent: This activity gives your child practice with dictionary skills.

Reading an index

Use the index below to answer the questions at the bottom of the page.

Index

Apes	10	Kangaroos	20
Bears	8	Monkeys	6
Chimpanzees	14	Penguins	28
Crocodiles	22	Sharks	4
Dolphins	26	Turtles	12
Giraffes	18	Whales	16

Page 18 is about _____

Page 28 is about _____

Page 16 is about _____

Page 8 is about _____

Page 12 is about _____

Apes are on page _____

Sharks are on page _____

Kangaroos are on page _____

Giraffes are on page _____

Chimpanzees are on page _____

Which page would you like to read? _____

Why? _____

_____

Making word banks

Write the words in the correct lists.

Things I eat	Things I see on wheels

sandwich

van

egg

train

bicycle

apple

car

grapes

bus

banana

Write the words in the correct lists.

Things I use in the kitchen	Things I use in the garden

spade

pan

knife

wheelbarrow

frying pan

watering can

spoon

fork

food processor

lawnmower

Note for parent: Word banks are useful for your child to keep and use for independent writing.

31

Words and sentences

Make two more words by adding one letter.

ball   **__all**   **__all**

Write a sentence with each of the two words you have made.

1._____

2._____

Now do the same again with these words.

man   **__an**   **__an**

hat   **__at**   **__at**

1._____

2._____

1._____

2._____

Note for parent: As well as spelling simple words, this activity encourages your child's independent writing skills.

Find the rhymes

Colour in blue the words that rhyme with **take**.
Colour in green the words that rhyme with **ball**.
Colour in red the words that rhyme with **shell**.
Colour in yellow the words that rhyme with **pin**.

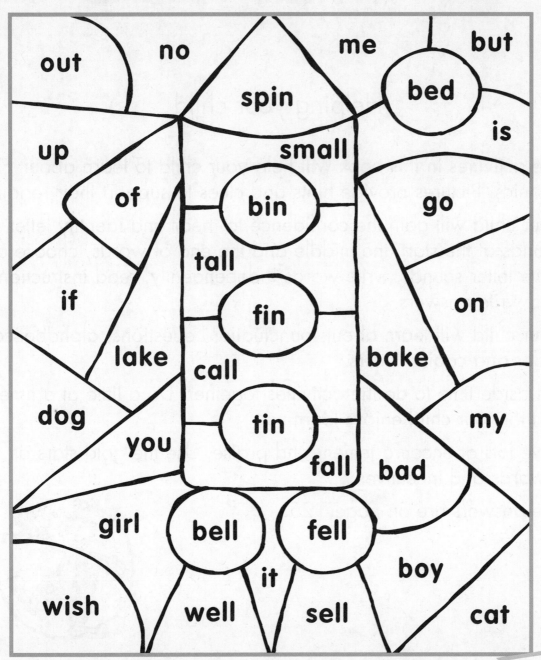

Note for parent: This activity encourages your child to look for patterns in words.

33

Phonics

Helping your child

⭐ The activities in this book will help your child to learn about phonics. Pictures provide hints and clues to support their reading.

⭐ Your child will gain the confidence to: hear and identify letter sounds at the start, the middle and the end of words, choose and write letter sounds, write words independently, read instructions and write answers.

⭐ Your child will learn about: punctuation, questions, alphabetical order and capital letters.

⭐ Set aside time to do the activities together. Do a little at a time so that your child enjoys learning.

⭐ Give lots of encouragement and praise. Use the gold stars as rewards and incentives.

⭐ The answers are on page 125.

Contents

Letter sounds a to z

Write in the missing letters of the alphabet.
Draw in the missing pictures.
Practise saying each word and letter sound.

A is for apple.

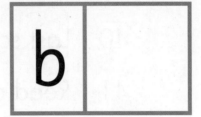

B is for ball.

C is for cat.

D is for duck.

E is for elephant.

F is for fish.

G is for gate.

H is for hat.

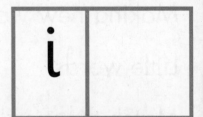

I is for igloo.

J is for jar.

K is for king.

L is for ladybird.

Note for parent: This activity helps children with alphabetical order and letter sounds.

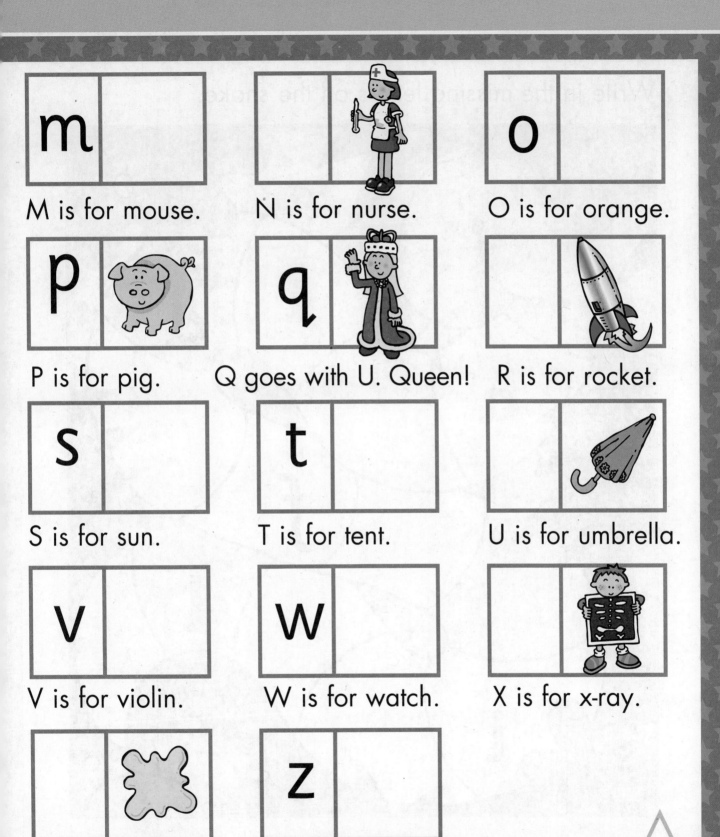

m

M is for mouse.

N is for nurse.

o

O is for orange.

p

P is for pig.

q

Q goes with U. Queen!

R is for rocket.

s

S is for sun.

t

T is for tent.

U is for umbrella.

V

V is for violin.

W

W is for watch.

X is for x-ray.

Y is for yellow.

Z

Z is for zebra.

Write in the missing letters on the snake.

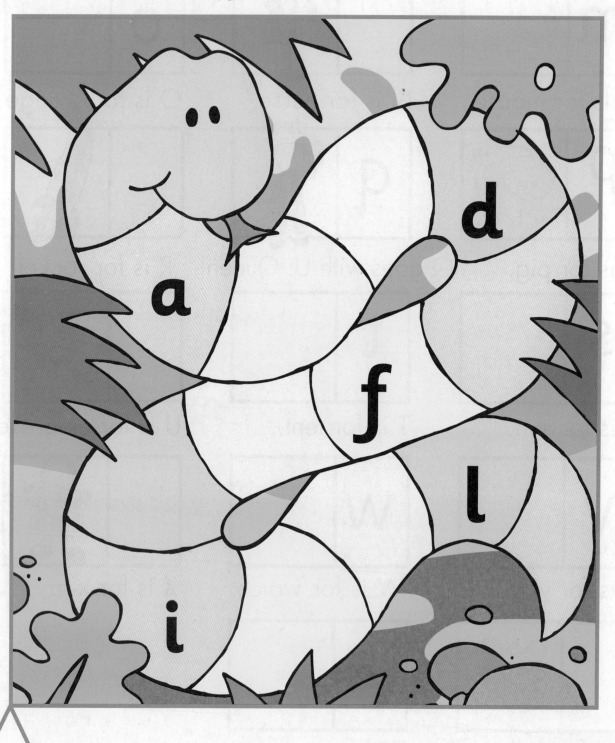

Note for parent: This activity helps children to practise lower-case alphabetical order without picture reference.

Write in the missing letters on the rollercoaster.

Word endings

Draw lines to join the words that have the same endings.

ball

balloon

bee

nail

carrot

tree

snail

wall

moon

parrot

Note for parent: Encourage your child to say each word and underline the matching word endings.

Consonant blends

Write over the beginning sound in each word.

 **fl**ag

 **cl**own

 **dr**agon

 **sp**oon

Now choose a sound to write at the beginning of these words.

dr	fl	gr	sp	cl

 __ **o c k**

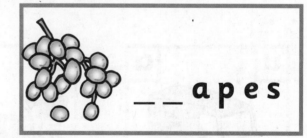 __ **a p e s**

 __ **o w e r**

 __ **u m**

Note for parent: This activity helps children to begin to recognize consonant blends and how to use them.

41

Middle sounds

Draw a circle around the correct middle sounds.

Bedroom words

Can you spot these things in the big picture? Draw a line to join each word to the right object.

br – brush   **fl – flowers**

sc – scarf   **bl – blankets**   **cr – crayons**

tr – triangle   **dr – drum**

gl – glove   **cl – clock**

Note for parent: This activity gives further practice with consonant blends, placing them in an everyday scene your child will recognize.

Read the words in the boxes. Then find them in the big words. Draw a circle around each one you find. The first one has been done for you.

too	he	one	or
up	on	she	an

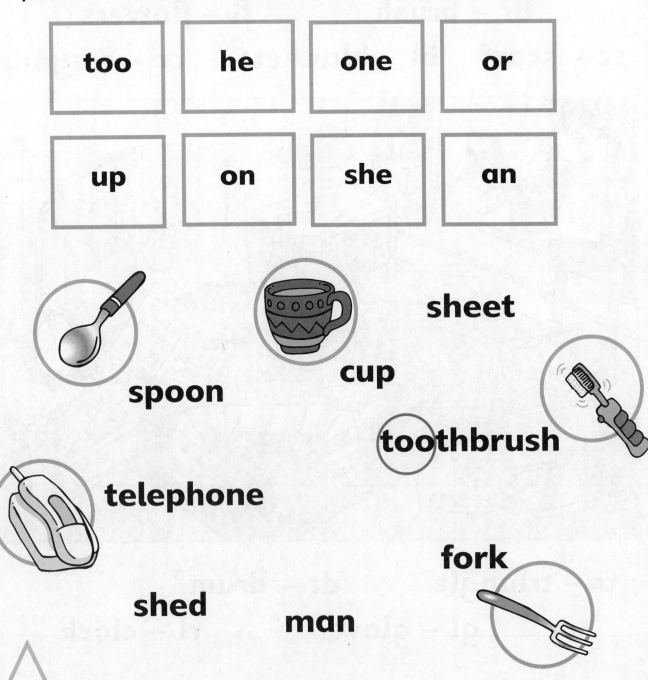

spoon

cup

sheet

toothbrush

telephone

shed

man

fork

Fill in the missing letters and pictures. You can choose your own pictures.

Choose one of these beginning sounds to complete the words in the boxes.

dr   sp   cl

__ __ a g o n

__ __ o w n

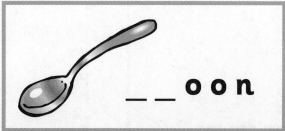

__ __ o o n

Note for parent: This is a revision of some of the learning covered so far.

45

Making new words

Write the new words you make.

Change the **b** in **bat**  to make c _ _

Change the **f** in **fox**  to make b _ _

Change the **j** in **jar**  to make c _ _

Change the **d** in **dog**  to make l _ _

Now draw a picture of each new word and write them in the boxes below.

Note for parent: This activity gives your child the opportunity to build words.

Little words

How many little words can you find in each big word?
Write the little words in the boxes.

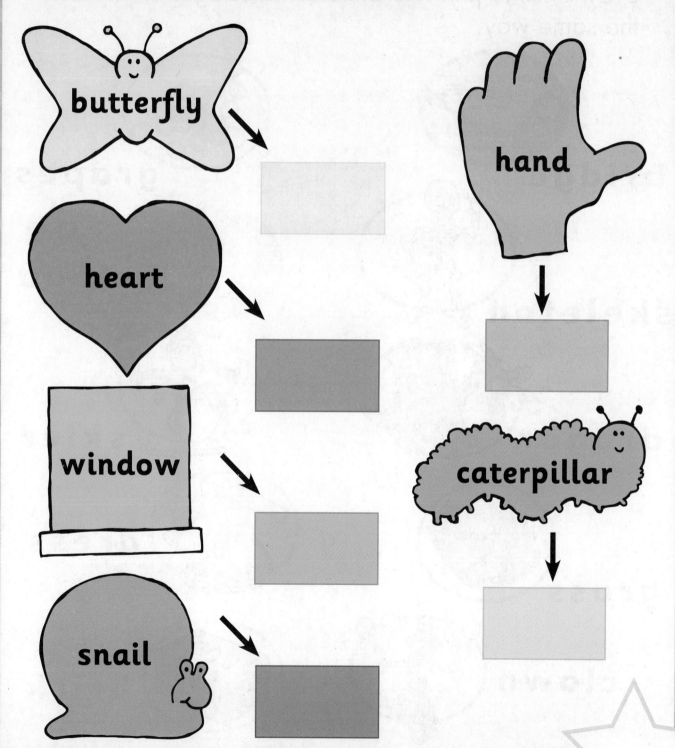

Note for parent: This activity gives further practice in identifying words within words.

47

Match the words

Look at the pictures and say the words.
Draw lines to join two pictures that begin in
the same way.

bridge

grapes

skeleton

cloud

dragon

skier

grass

dress

clown

brick

Note for parent: This activity gives further practice with consonant blends, showing how they
can be used to form different words that start in the same way.

Choose one of these double sounds to complete the words below.

fr   sl   sp   cl   tr   tw

 _ _ o c k

 _ _ i d e

 _ _ a i n

 _ _ i d e r

 _ _ i n s

 _ _ o g

Note for parent: This activity gives your child further practice with using consonant blends.

49

Alphabetical order

abcdefghijklmnopqrstuvwxyz

Write the beginning sound of each picture. Then put the three letters in each row into alphabetical order. The first row has been done for you.

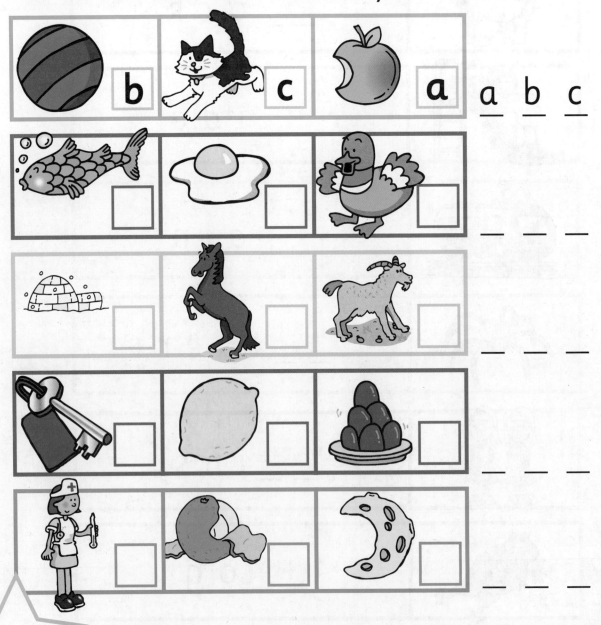

Note for parent: This activity combines letter sounds with alphabetical order.

Look at the pictures and write the words.
The words in the box will help you.

globe bread frog flag grapes blue plug

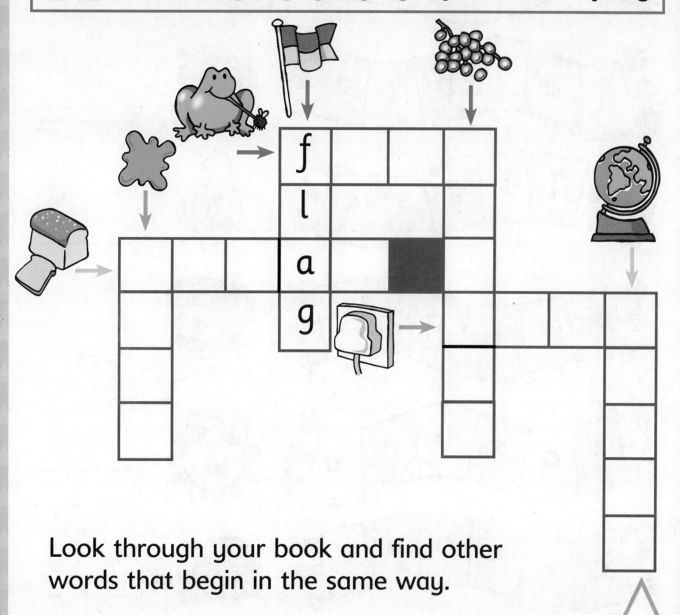

Look through your book and find other
words that begin in the same way.

Hidden words

Find a word inside each scarf. Write the words in the spaces. The first one has been done for you.

b u s

_ _ _

_ _ _

_ _ _

_ _ _

_ _ _

Note for parent: Focus on the first letter sound when looking for each hidden word.

Describing

What are these sentences describing?

Choose a word to write at the end of each one.

| shorts   sheep   shark   shoes   ship   shell |

1. This sails across the sea. _ _ _ _

2. You find this on a farm. _ _ _ _ _

3. You wear these on your feet. _ _ _ _ _

4. This fish has very sharp teeth. _ _ _ _ _

5. You find this on the beach. _ _ _ _ _

6. You wear these in the summer. _ _ _ _ _ _

Last sounds in words

Say the name of each picture. Write the last letter sound at the end of each word.

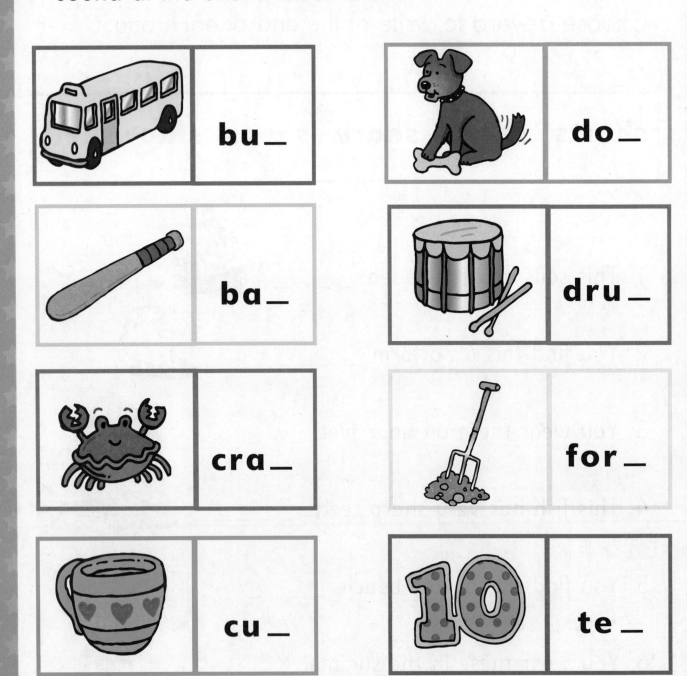

bu _

do _

ba _

dru _

cra _

for _

cu _

te _

Note for parent: Children need to listen carefully to identify last letters.

Tick each box as you spot these things in the picture.

Find two things that begin with **ch**. ☐ ☐

Find two things that begin with **tr**. ☐ ☐

Find two things that begin with **str**. ☐ ☐

Find two things that begin with **sw**. ☐ ☐

Find two things that begin with **dr**. ☐ ☐

Find two things that begin with **cr**. ☐ ☐

Note for parent: As well as reading, your child is learning about consonant blends ch, tr, str, sw, dr and cr.

Find the animal

Colour in brown all the words beginning with **br**.
Colour in red all the words beginning with **dr**.
Colour in yellow all the words beginning with **st**.
Colour in green all the words beginning with **gl**.
Colour in blue all the words beginning with **sk**.
Colour in purple all the words beginning with **tr**.

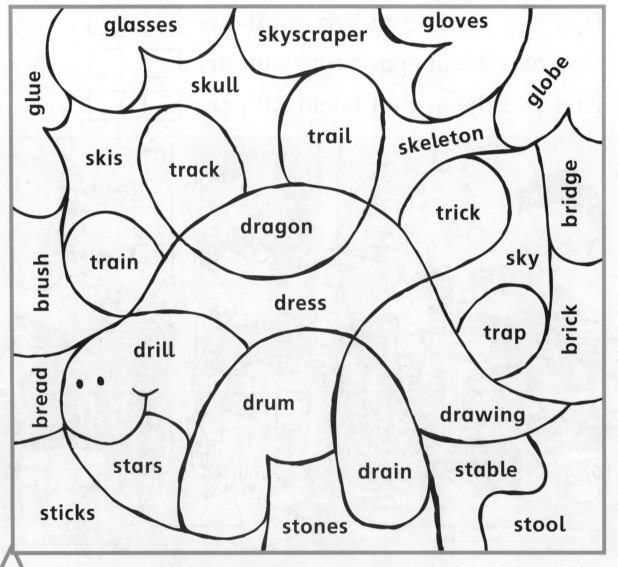

Which animal can you see?

More than one

You add the letter **s** when there is more than one. Write the whole words in the spaces.

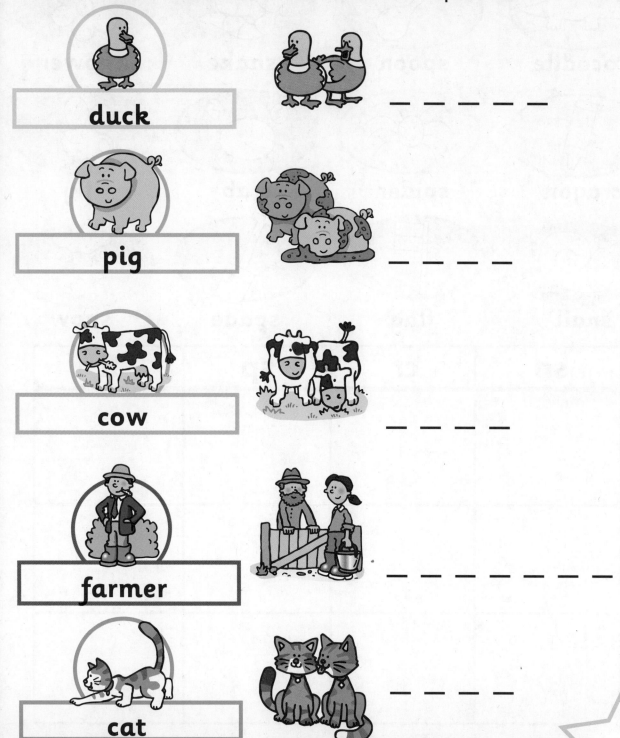

duck

_ _ _ _ _

pig

_ _ _ _

cow

_ _ _ _

farmer

_ _ _ _ _ _ _

cat

_ _ _ _

Note for parent: This activity helps children to learn about plurals.

57

Sorting

Draw each picture in the correct box.

crocodile

spoon

snake

flower

crayon

spider

crab

fly

snail

flag

spade

snow

sn	cr	sp	fl

Note for parent: As well as sorting, your child is seeing and reading words with the consonant blends sn, cr, sp and fl.

Quick quiz

What are these sentences describing?

Choose a word to write at the end of each one.

> ## sheep   shell   ship

1. This sails across the sea. _ _ _ _

2. You find this on a farm. _ _ _ _ _

3. You find this on the beach. _ _ _ _ _

Add the letter **s** when there is more than one.
Write the whole words in the spaces.

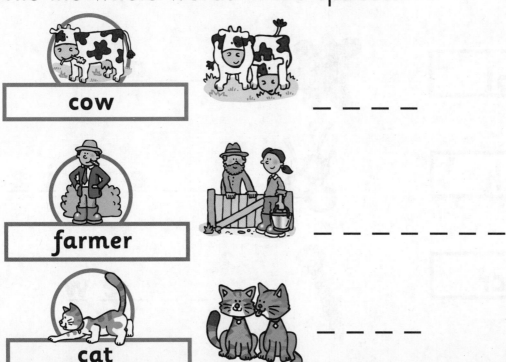

cow

_ _ _ _

farmer

_ _ _ _ _ _ _

cat

_ _ _ _

Note for parent: This is a quick revision of some of the learning covered so far.

59

Make a word

Choose a beginning to write at the start of each word. Say each picture name out loud before you start.

str		_ _ _ <u>i n</u> g
tr		_ _ <u>a i n</u>
gl		_ _ <u>a s s e s</u>
bl		_ _ <u>a c k</u>
ch		_ _ <u>e r r i e s</u>
scr		_ _ _ <u>e w</u>

Write the last sound in each word. Choose from this list. Draw a line to join the words that have the same ending.

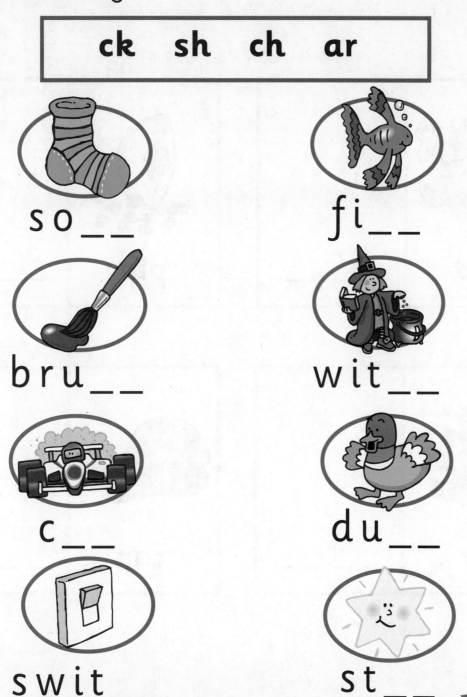

ck   sh   ch   ar

so_ _

fi_ _

bru_ _

wit_ _

c _ _

du_ _

swit_ _

st_ _

Note for parent: This activity helps your child to learn about the word endings ck, sh, ch and ar.

61

Adding the letter e

Add the letter **e** to the end of each word to make a new word. Write the new word and draw a picture of it.

cub   _ _ _ _

pip   _ _ _ _

fir   _ _ _ _

cap   _ _ _ _

Note for parent: This activity helps your child understand what happens to a vowel sound inside a word, when an e is added to the end.

Groups of words

Some words belong together.
Write these words into the correct group.

car   lion   bread   apple

bus

banana   tiger

giraffe   train

transport

_____
_____
_____

animals

_____
_____
_____

food

_____
_____
_____

Note for parent: Make more word groups of things that interest your child to give
them extra writing practice.

Maths

Helping your child

⭐ The activities in this book will help your child to learn about maths. Pictures provide hints and clues to support your child's understanding.

⭐ Your child will gain the confidence to: count to 20, add and take away, identify a range of 2D and 3D shapes, begin to tell the time and order, group and measure objects.

⭐ Your child will learn about: numbers, shapes, halves, sets and pairs.

⭐ Set aside time to do the activities together. Do a little at a time so that your child enjoys learning.

⭐ Give lots of encouragement and praise. Use the gold stars as rewards and incentives.

⭐ The answers are on page 126.

Contents

Write the numbers. Join each picture to
the right number. Join each number
to the right word.

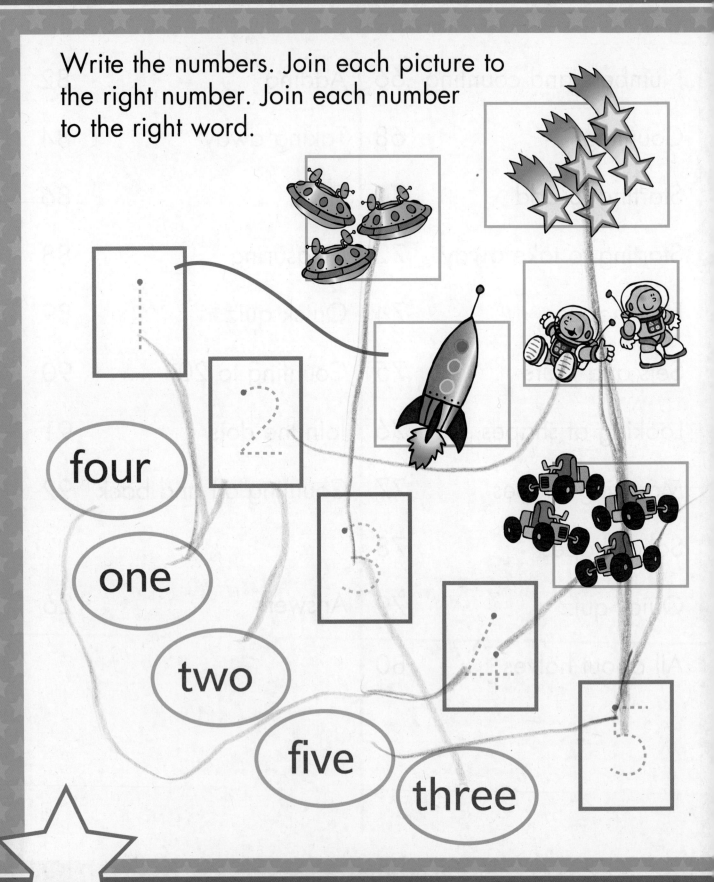

four

one

two

five

three

Note for parent: Ask your child to say each number and word aloud as he or she traces over them.

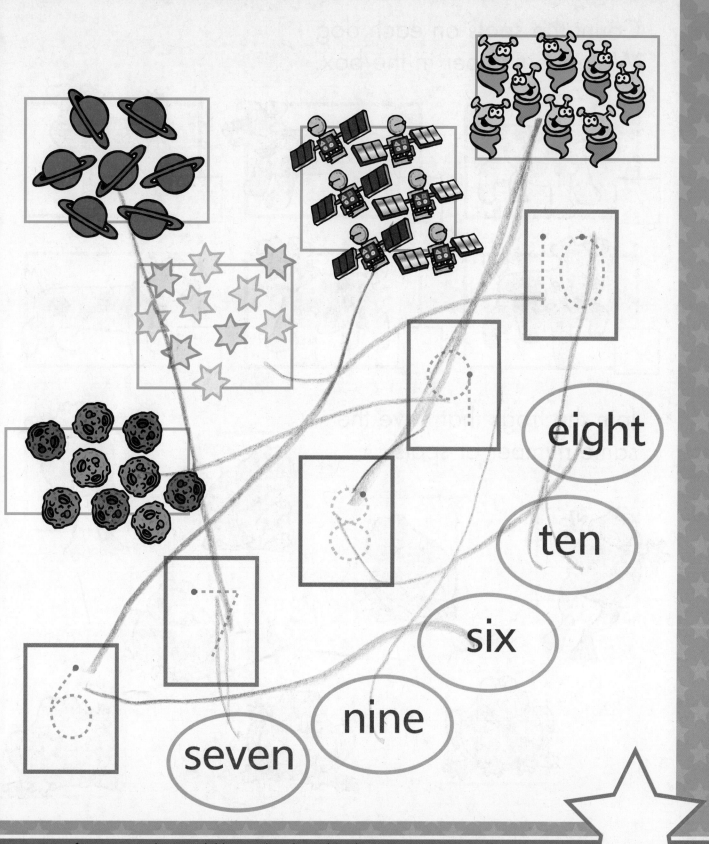

Note for parent: Help your child to work with numbers by saying a number and asking them what number is one more/less.

67

Counting

Count the spots on each dog.
Write the number in the box.

Join the frogs that have the
same number of spots.

Note for parent: This activity gives practice in using counting skills in different ways.

Each frog needs 10 spots.
Draw in the missing spots.

Join the pairs of dogs. Each pair must
have a total of 10 spots.

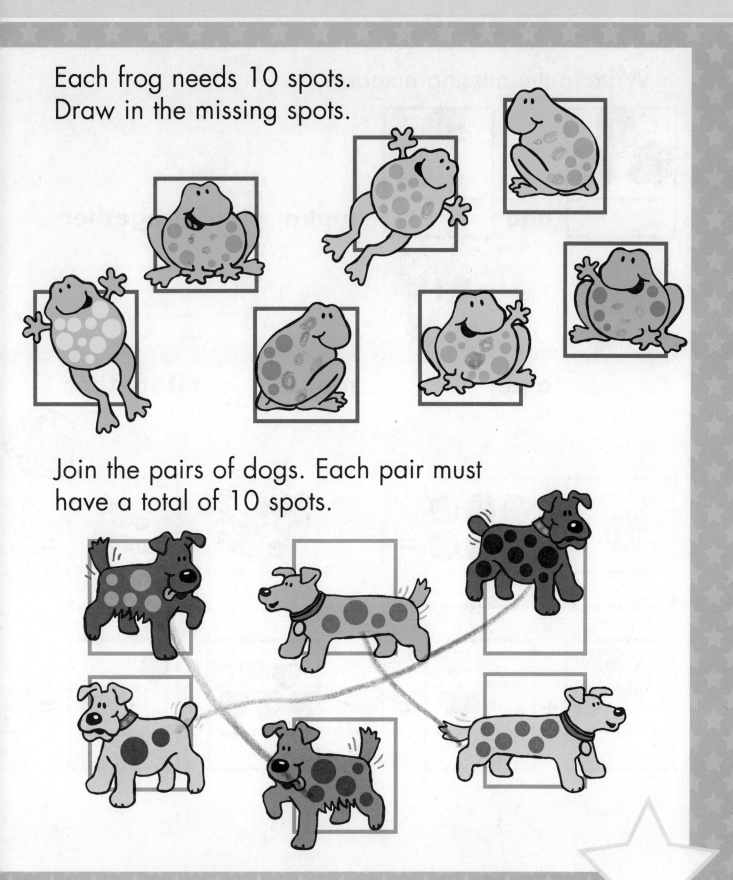

Note for parent: Help your child to write down all the pairs of numbers that add up to 10.

69

Starting to add

Write in the missing numbers.

 and  make 5 altogether

 and  make 6 altogether

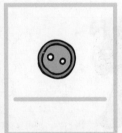 + = 7  + 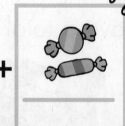 = 7

 + = 7  +  = 9

Note for parent: In this activity your child is adding with objects, which helps to prepare them for adding with numbers.

Draw the missing socks above each arrow.

| **1** | + | **4** | = | **5** |

| **2** | + | **3** | = | **5** |

| **3** | + | **4** | = | **7** |

| **4** | + | **3** | = | **7** |

Write the missing numbers.

| 3 | + | **5** | = | **8** |

| 4 | + | **4** | = | **8** |

| 1 | + | **5** | = | **6** |

| 2 | + | **5** | = | **7** |

Starting to take away

Dino the dinosaur eats 2 of everything he sees.
Cross out how many pieces of food Dino eats.
Write how many are left after Dino has eaten.

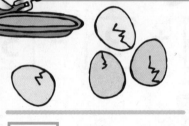

4 take away **2**

leaves 2

6 take away **2**

leaves 4

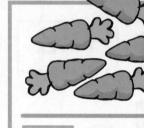

5 take away **2**

leaves 3

8 take away **2**

leaves 6

7 take away **2**

leaves 5

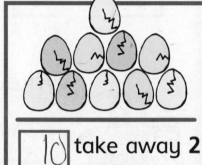

10 take away **2**

leaves 8

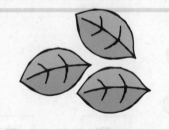

3 – 2 = 1

2 – 2 = 0

9 – 2 = 7

Note for parent: Taking away is a first step towards learning about subtraction.

How many fish has Charlie the cat eaten from each bowl? Join each START bowl to the correct FINISH bowl.

START

FINISH

take away **2**

take away **1**

take away **2**

take away **2**

take away **3**

take away **6**

Flat shapes

Cross the odd one out in each ring.

Tick all the shapes that are the same in each row.

Note for parent: Recognizing common shapes is a key part of maths teaching for your child at this age.

Sets and pairs

Join each set of shapes to its name.

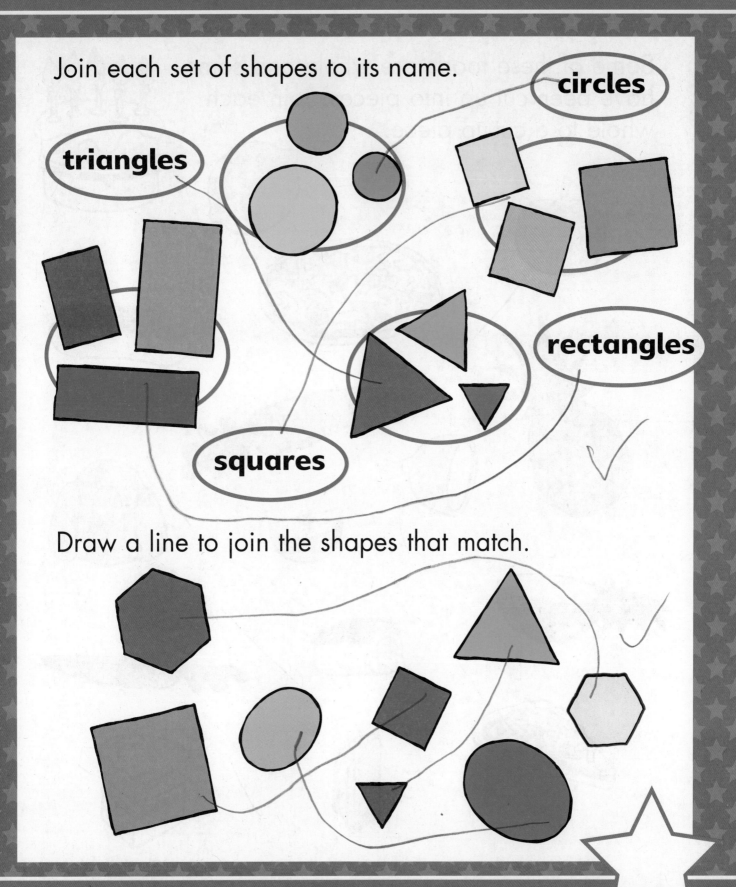

circles

triangles

rectangles

squares

Draw a line to join the shapes that match.

Note for parent: Gradually your child should learn the names of common shapes.

75

Looking at shapes

Some of these foods are whole and some have been cut up into pieces. Join each whole to a cut-up piece.

Note for parent: This activity encourages your child to examine shapes closely. Ask your child if they can group the items by a different criterion – e.g. sweet or savoury, fruit or vegetable.

Matching shapes

Colour the matching shapes.

 colour red   colour green

 colour blue   colour orange

Solid shapes

Join each set of shapes to its name.

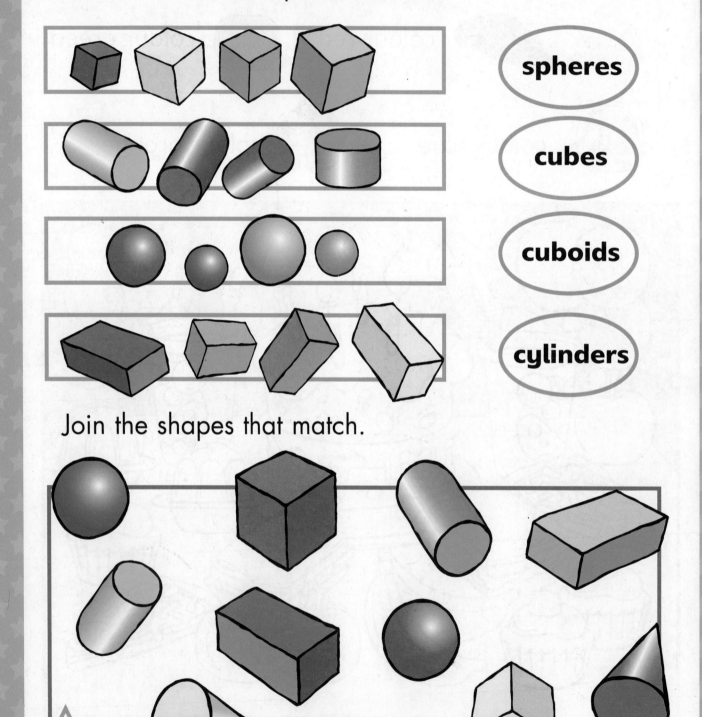

spheres

cubes

cuboids

cylinders

Join the shapes that match.

Note for parent: Ask your child to find examples of these solid shapes around the home. Ask them to recall the shape names as they become familiar to your child.

Join each START food to the correct FINISH food.

 START

add on **0**

 add on **3**

 add on **6**

 add on **6**

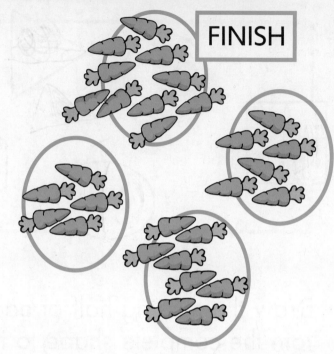 FINISH

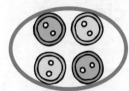 START

take away **3**

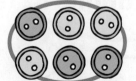 take away **2**

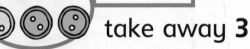 take away **0**

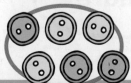 take away **5**

Join each START group to the correct FINISH group.

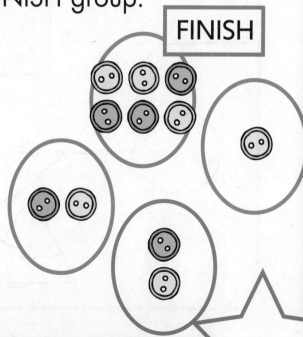 FINISH

Note for parent: This activity helps your child to remember about adding and taking away.

79

Colour half of each shape.

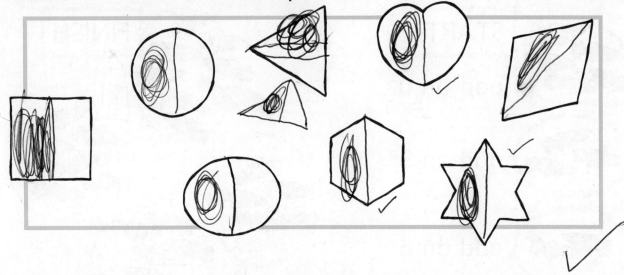

Draw the missing half of each shape.
Join the complete shape to its name.

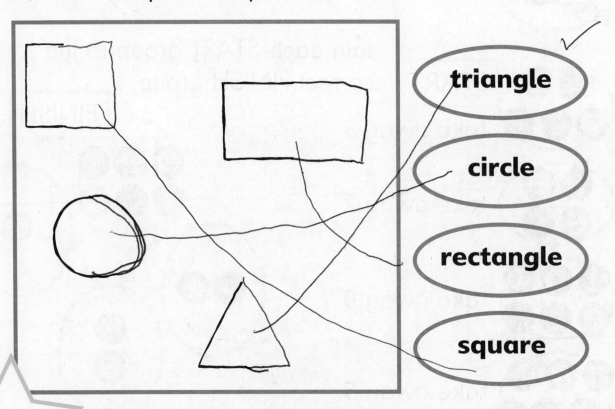

triangle

circle

rectangle

square

Note for parent: Learning about half and fair shares is important in mathematics.

Colour half of the items in
each container.

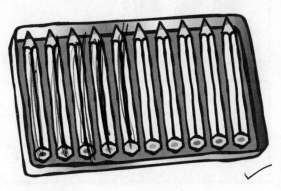

Some marbles are put into two bags.
Put a tick (✔) if the sharing is fair.
Put a cross (✘) if the sharing is not fair.

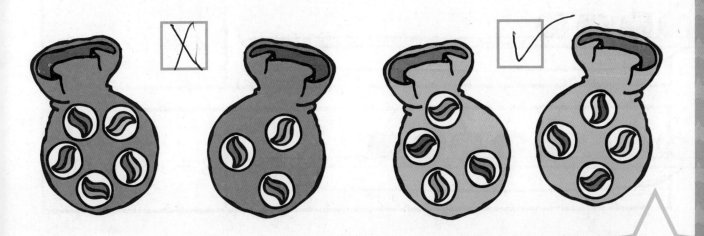

Note for parent: Encourage your child to practise sharing real-life objects equally. Sweets
and coins of the same value are good examples to use.

81

Adding

Draw in the extra crayons.
Write the total number of crayons.

 1 add **4**

$1 + 4 = 5$

 **3** add **3**

$3 + 3 = 6$

 **4** add **6**

$4 + 6 = 10$

There should be 10 cherries on each plate. Draw the missing cherries.

$4 + 6 = 10$

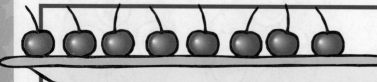

$8 + 2 = 10$

Note for parent: Your child may need to use the number track on page 83 to complete these additions.

Use the number track to help you.
Write how many beads are on each necklace.

4 + 3 = 7

6 + 2 = 8

2 + 5 = 7

3 + 3 = 6

1 + 5 = 6

6 + 3 = 9

Join the scarves that have the same total.

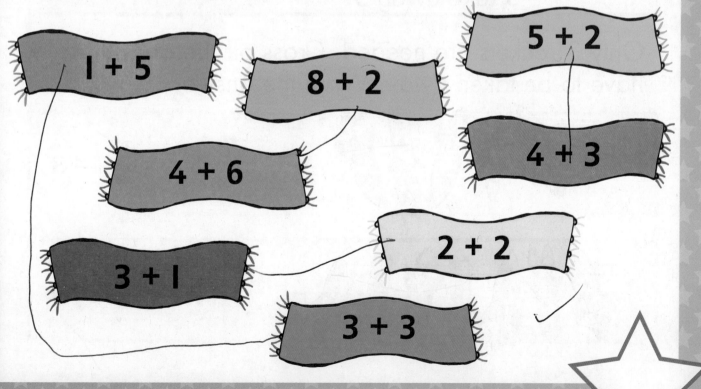

1 + 5

8 + 2

5 + 2

4 + 6

4 + 3

3 + 1

2 + 2

3 + 3

Taking away

Cross off the animals to be taken away.
Write how many are left.

4 take away 2

$4 - 2 = 2$

7 take away 3

$7 - 3 = 4$

8 take away 5

$8 - 5 = 3$

Only 3 rockets are needed. Cross off the ones that have to be taken away. Write the answer.

$5 - 2 = 3$

$7 - 4 = 3$

Note for parent: Your child may need to use the number track on page 85 to complete these subtractions.

Use the number track to help you answer
the subtractions.

4 – 1 = 3

5 – 3 = 2

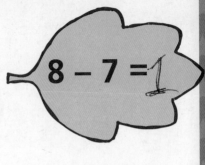
8 – 7 = 1

5 – 5 = 0

9 – 5 = 4

10 – 2 = 8

Join the stars that have the same answer.

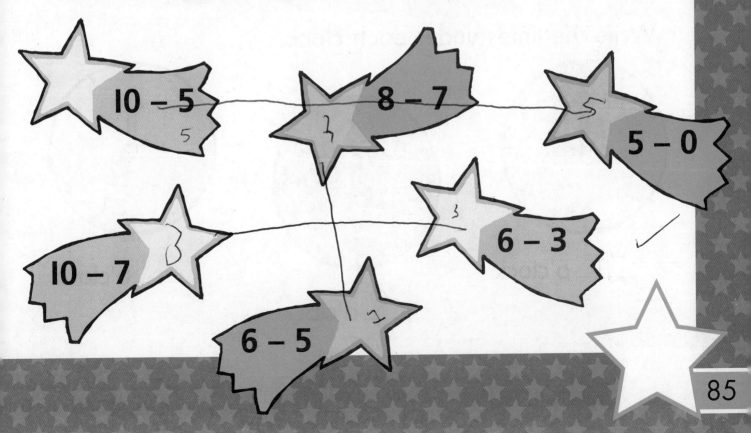

10 – 5
5

8 – 7
1

5

5 – 0

10 – 7
3

3

6 – 3

6 – 5
1

85

Time

Write in the missing numbers on the clock.

Write the times under each clock.

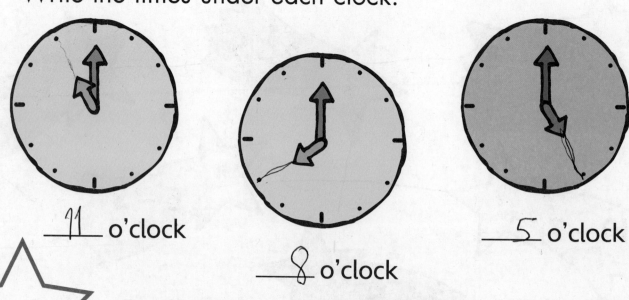

_11_ o'clock

_8_ o'clock

_5_ o'clock

Note for parent: This activity will help your child to start recognizing simple times.

Look at the times. Draw in the missing hands.

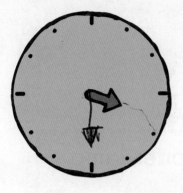

half-past 3

half-past 8

half-past 12

Write the times under each clock.

half-past __4__

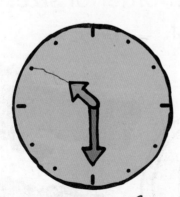

half-past __16__

half-past __7__ ✓

Note for parent: For further practice with the concept of time, ask your child if they can name the days of the week and the months of the year.

87

Measuring

Draw a longer worm.

Draw a bigger flower.

Draw a taller rocket.

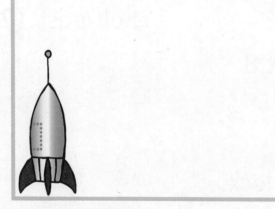

Draw a shorter lamp post.

Join up the pictures in order of size.
Start with the smallest.

Note for parent: In this activity your child is learning to estimate and compare measurements.

Quick quiz

Use the number track to help you write the answers.

0 1 2 3 4 5 6 7 8 9 10

$2 + 4 =$

$3 + 3 =$

$5 + 4 =$

$6 + 4 =$

$5 + 5 =$

$2 + 3 =$

$1 + 7 =$

$2 + 7 =$

$2 + 2 =$

$10 - 1 =$

$5 - 3 =$

$4 - 2 =$

$8 - 3 =$

$6 - 5 =$

$10 - 6 =$

$7 - 4 =$

$9 - 6 =$

$7 - 2 =$

Note for parent: Encourage children to look back through the book if they need
help with the answers.

89

Write in the missing numbers.

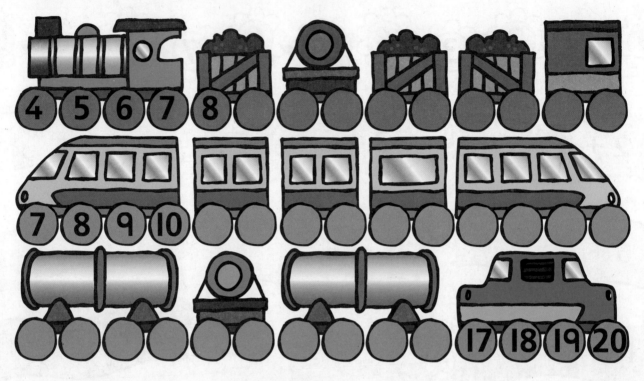

Join each word to a number.

12

16

15

20

11

17

14

13

eleven   twenty

fourteen   sixteen

twelve   thirteen

fifteen   seventeen

Note for parent: This activity gives your child practice in counting to 20, and in recognizing numbers and words.

Join the dots in order.
Can you name the mystery animals?

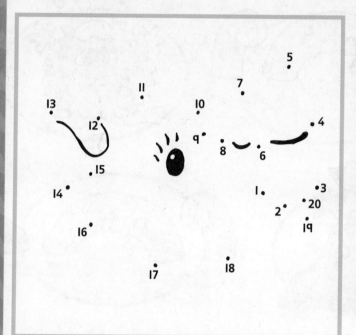

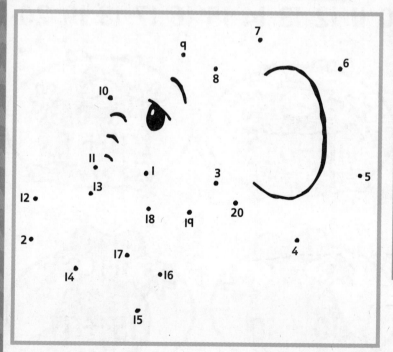

Note for parent: This activity gives further practice in counting up to 20.

91

Counting on and back

Use the number track to help you count on.
Join each monster to its correct answer on the track.

8 + 3

9 + 5

8 + 7

6 + 7

9 + 9

6 + 4

0 1 2 3 4 5 6 7 8 9 10 11 12 13 14 15 16 17 18 19 20

10 + 3

10 + 5

10 + 8

12 + 6

10 + 10

15 + 1

Note for parent: This activity will help your child to use a number track to count on and back.
Encourage your child to count on in twos and fives along the number track.

Use the number track to help you count back. Join each spaceship to its correct answer on the track.

0 1 2 3 4 5 6 7 8 9 10 11 12 13 14 15 16 17 18 19 20

Note for parent: Encourage your child to count back in twos and fives along the number track.

93

Adding and taking away

Helping your child

⭐ The activities in this book will help your child to learn about adding and taking away. Pictures provide hints and clues to support your child's calculations.

⭐ Your child will gain the confidence to: read, write and identify numbers to 20, use a number line to count on and back, add and take away one-digit numbers to and from each other, understand the +, − and = symbols and calculate the value of an unknown number within a number sentence.

⭐ Your child will learn about: numbers to 20, adding and subtracting bonds, counting, comparing and differences.

⭐ Set aside time to do the activities together. Do a little at a time so that your child enjoys learning.

⭐ Give lots of encouragement and praise.
Use the gold stars as rewards and incentives.

⭐ The answers are on page 127.

Contents

Numbers to 10

Trace the numbers. Join each kite to the right number. Join each number to the right group of pictures at the bottom of each page.

Note for parent: Ask your child to say each number and word aloud as he or she traces over them.

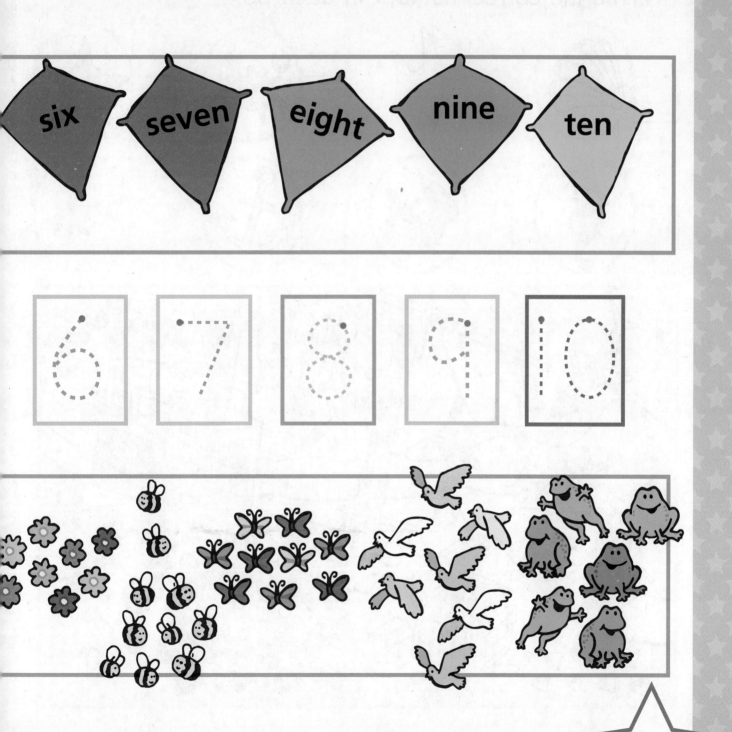

six seven eight nine ten

6 7 8 9 10

Note for parent: Help your child to work with numbers by saying a number and
asking them what number is one more/less.

97

Counting

Count the objects in the big picture.
Write the correct number in each box.

Note for parent: To help find the totals, your child can mark each object as they count.

Comparing

Colour most spaceships red. Colour the rest of the spaceships blue. Write the numbers in the boxes.

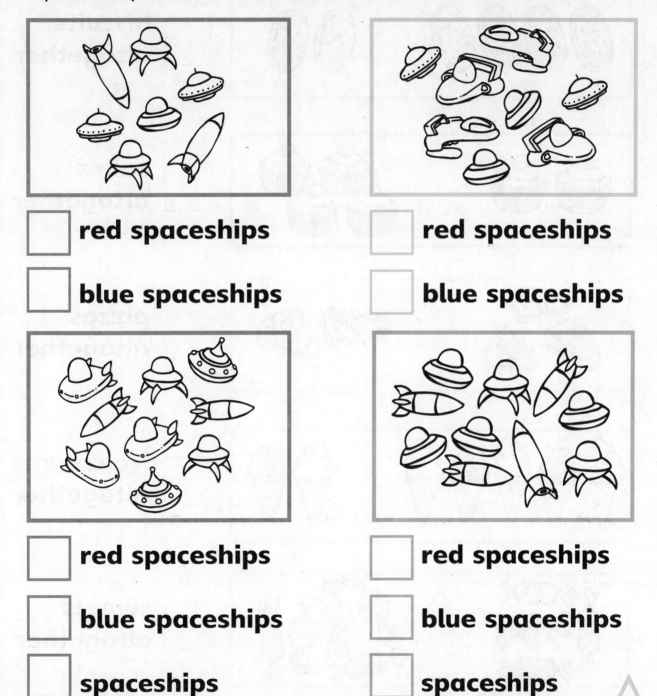

☐ **red spaceships**	☐ **red spaceships**
☐ **blue spaceships**	☐ **blue spaceships**
☐ **red spaceships**	☐ **red spaceships**
☐ **blue spaceships**	☐ **blue spaceships**
☐ **spaceships altogether**	☐ **spaceships altogether**

Note for parent: Your child can choose the number of spaceships to colour red, but there must be more red spaceships than blue ones.

99

Putting together

Count each set. Write how many there are altogether.

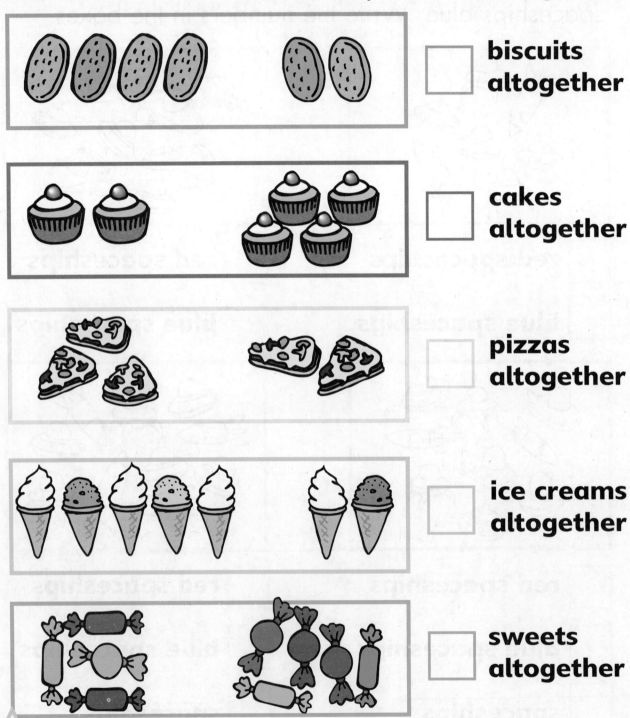

biscuits
altogether

cakes
altogether

pizzas
altogether

ice creams
altogether

sweets
altogether

Note for parent: Encourage your child to count on from the first number to find the total.

Count the spots on each monster.
How many spots are there altogether?

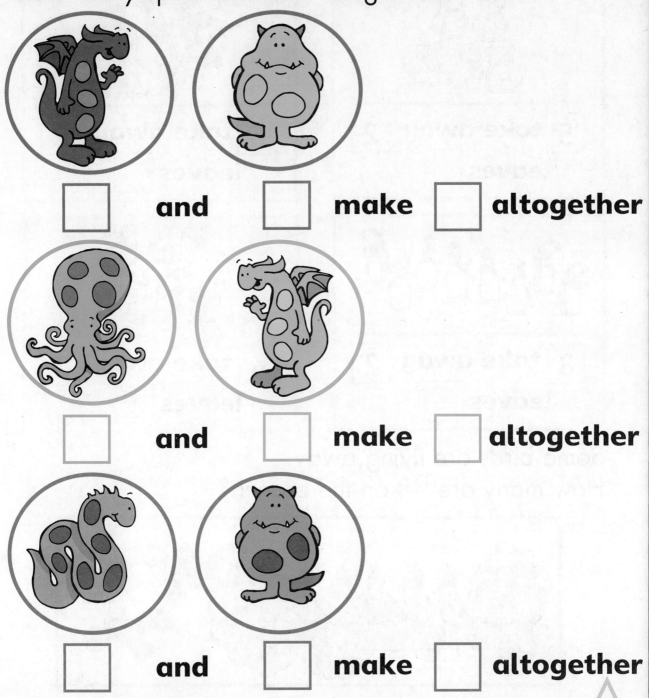

[   ] **and** [   ] **make** [   ] **altogether**

[   ] **and** [   ] **make** [   ] **altogether**

[   ] **and** [   ] **make** [   ] **altogether**

How many are left?

Cross out two in each set. Write how many are left.

5 take away 2

leaves ☐

6 take away 2

leaves ☐

8 take away 2

leaves ☐

4 take away 2

leaves ☐

Some birds are flying away.
How many are left on the branch?

9 take away 3 leaves ☐

Note for parent: This activity will help your child begin to understand the idea of taking away (subtracting).

Finding differences

How many more children are there than chairs?

☐ **children**

☐ **chairs**

difference → ☐

☐ **children**

☐ **chairs**

difference → ☐

☐ **children**

☐ **chairs**

difference → ☐

Note for parent: Finding the difference is the same as counting up
from the smaller number to the larger one.

Number machines

Sweets go into these adding machines.
Write how many come out of each machine.

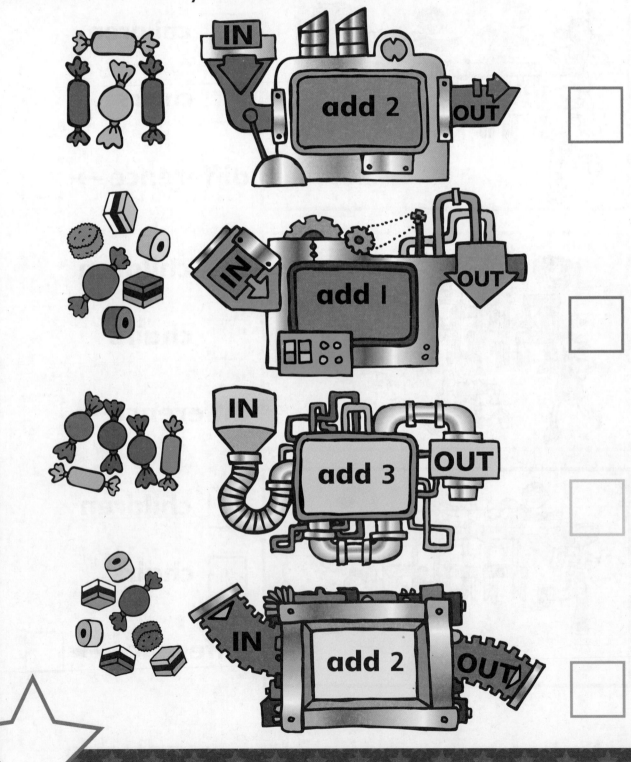

Note for parent: Encourage your child to count on from the IN number
for adding, and to count back for taking away.

Drinks go into these take-away machines.
Write how many come out of each machine.

Count each set. Write how many there are altogether.

☐ **biscuits altogether**

☐ **cakes altogether**

Count the spots on each monster. How many are there altogether?

☐ **and** ☐ **make** ☐ **altogether**

Cross out two in each set. Write how many are left.

8 **take away** 2

leaves ☐

4 **take away** 2

leaves ☐

Note for parent: This page helps to find out what your child can remember.

Numbers to 20

Join each word to a number.

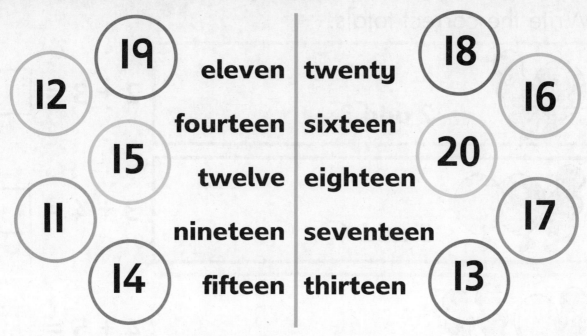

19 12 15 11 14

eleven | twenty
fourteen | sixteen
twelve | eighteen
nineteen | seventeen
fifteen | thirteen

18 16 20 17 13

Complete the number table.

eleven	11
	12
thirteen	
fourteen	
	15
sixteen	
	17
	18
nineteen	
	20

Group the numbers by their colour circles above.

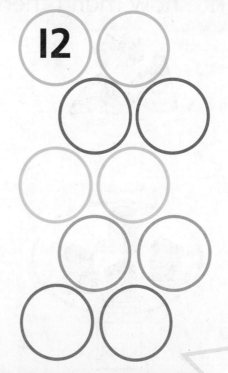

12

Note for parent: Solving problems using tables and sorting numbers using different criteria for grouping them are important maths skills for your child at this age.

Adding

Draw the extra balloons in each row.
Write the correct totals.

 **2 add 3**

$2 + 3 =$ ☐

 **3 add 4**

$3 + 4 =$ ☐

 **4 add 5**

$4 + 5 =$ ☐

Write how many there are altogether.

☐ + ☐ = ☐

☐ + ☐ = ☐

Write how many coloured pencils there are altogether.

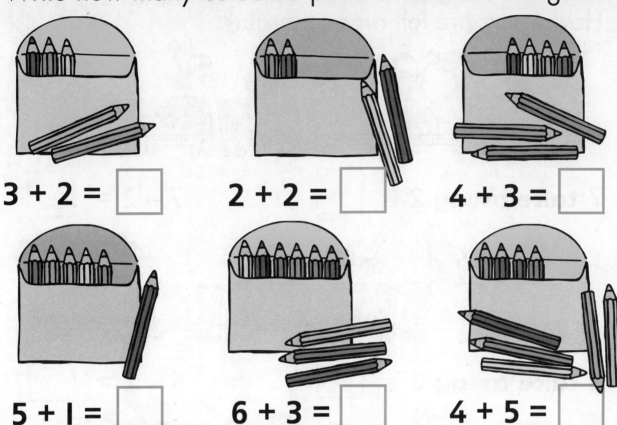

3 + 2 = ☐   2 + 2 = ☐   4 + 3 = ☐

5 + 1 = ☐   6 + 3 = ☐   4 + 5 = ☐

Join each sum to the correct total.

5 + 2   3 + 3   4 + 1   1 + 3   4 + 4

5   8   6   7   4

Taking away

Two children get out of each of these trains.
How many are left on each train?

7 take away 2 is ☐   **7 – 2 =** ☐

5 take away 2 is ☐   **5 – 2 =** ☐

8 take away 2 is ☐   **8 – 2 =** ☐

Cross out some flags. Write how many are left.

          9 – ☐ **is** ☐

Note for parent: Use the words 'subtract' and 'take away' with your child to help them to recognize and understand the subtraction sign (–).

Draw how many balls come out of the machines.
Write the totals in the red boxes.

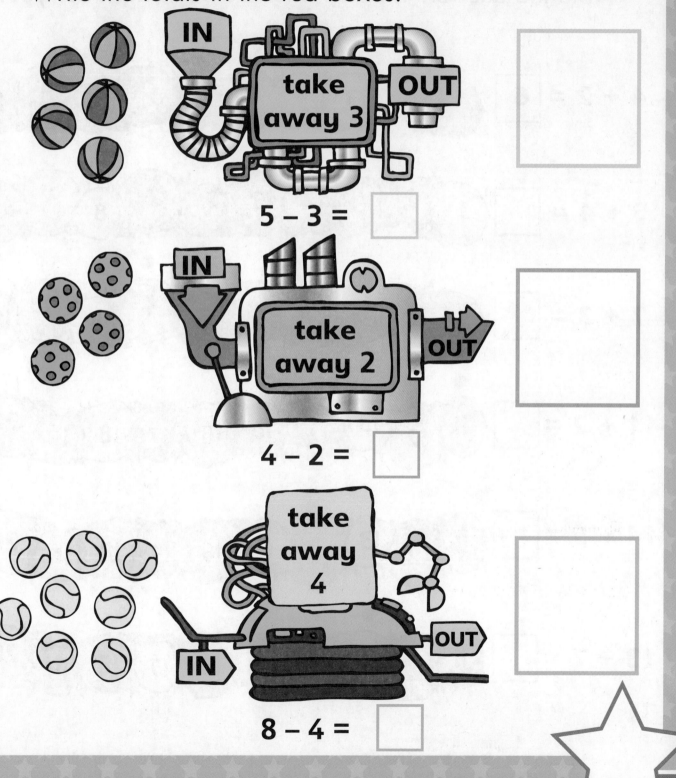

5 – 3 =

4 – 2 =

8 – 4 =

Counting on

Use the number track to count on. Show the jumps and write the answer. The first one has been done for you.

$4 + 2 = \boxed{6}$ 1 2 3 4 5 6 7 8 9 10

$5 + 4 = \boxed{}$ 1 2 3 4 5 6 7 8 9 10

$7 + 3 = \boxed{}$ 1 2 3 4 5 6 7 8 9 10

$11 + 2 = \boxed{}$ 11 12 13 14 15 16 17 18 19 20

$14 + 5 = \boxed{}$ 11 12 13 14 15 16 17 18 19 20

$13 + 7 = \boxed{}$ 11 12 13 14 15 16 17 18 19 20

Note for parent: This activity introduces adding to two-digit numbers. Encourage your child to count on in twos and fives along each number track.

Join each rocket to the correct answer on the number track.

1 2 3 4 5 6 7 8 9 10

5 + 2 =

3 + 3 =

3 + 1 =

4 + 1 =

6 + 3 =

Write the missing numbers in these counting patterns.

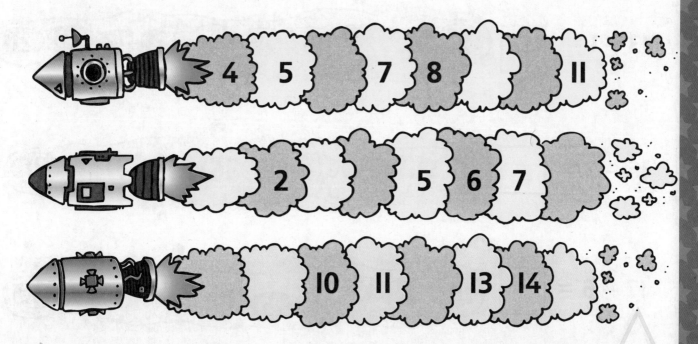

4 5 __ 7 8 __ __ 11

__ 2 __ __ 5 6 7

__ __ 10 11 __ 13 14

Counting back

Use the number track to count back. Show the jumps and write the answer.

6 – 3 = ☐

① ② ③ ④ ⑤ ⑥ ⑦ ⑧ ⑨ ⑩

5 – 2 = ☐

① ② ③ ④ ⑤ ⑥ ⑦ ⑧ ⑨ ⑩

8 – 4 = ☐

① ② ③ ④ ⑤ ⑥ ⑦ ⑧ ⑨ ⑩

13 – 1 = ☐

⑪ ⑫ ⑬ ⑭ ⑮ ⑯ ⑰ ⑱ ⑲ ⑳

16 – 3 = ☐

⑪ ⑫ ⑬ ⑭ ⑮ ⑯ ⑰ ⑱ ⑲ ⑳

17 – 6 = ☐

⑪ ⑫ ⑬ ⑭ ⑮ ⑯ ⑰ ⑱ ⑲ ⑳

Note for parent: This activity introduces subtracting from two-digit numbers. Encourage your child to count back in twos and fives along each number track.

Work out each answer. Colour the correct number in the number track to match.

Addition bonds

Make these totals in different ways.
Write the answers in the boxes.

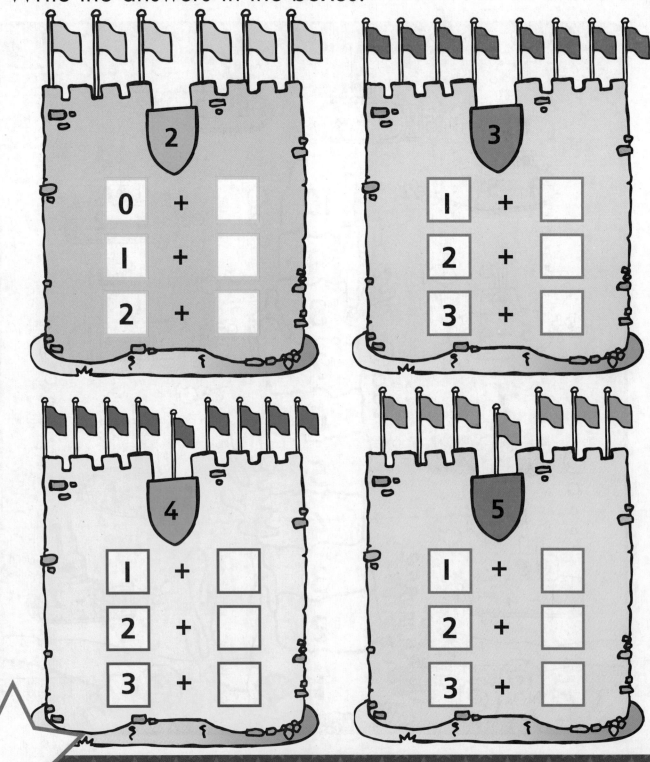

2

0 +
1 +
2 +

3

1 +
2 +
3 +

4

1 +
2 +
3 +

5

1 +
2 +
3 +

Note for parent: This activity helps your child to understand that numbers can be added in any order to achieve the same total. For example, 2 + 3 = 3 + 2 = 5.

Draw a line from each flower to the pot with the correct total.

6 + 3   6 + 2   8 + 2   3 + 5   5 + 4

7 + 3   4 + 6   8 + 1   4 + 4

8   9   10

What can you see if you colour all the shapes with a total of 10?

6 + 3   8 + 1   1 + 4   0 + 7   8 + 3

9 + 1   4 + 6   8 + 0

5 + 6   7 + 3   7 + 1

5 + 5   3 + 2

2 + 6   5 + 8   0 + 10   1 + 9

8 + 2   3 + 7

4 + 4   0 + 9   7 + 2   4 + 8

Subtraction bonds

Find different ways of making 1 and 2.

Find different ways to make the answer of 5.

Note for parent: Subtraction bonds with totals up to five bond pairs with a total of ten are key learning objectives for your child in this age group.

Join the sums to the correct totals.

Draw how many balls come out of the machines.

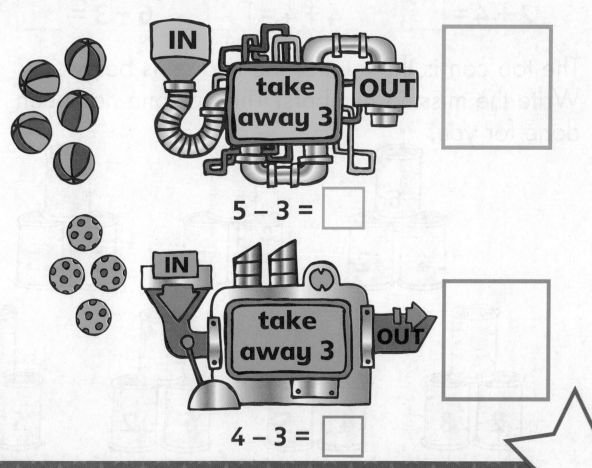

5 − 3 = ☐

4 − 3 = ☐

Note for parent: This page helps to find out what your child can remember.

119

Addition practice

Write the answers in the boxes. Use the number track to help you.

4 + 3 = ☐   6 + 2 = ☐   5 + 5 = ☐

9 + 1 = ☐   7 + 2 = ☐   3 + 5 = ☐

2 + 4 = ☐   4 + 4 = ☐   6 + 3 = ☐

The top can is the total of the two cans below. Write the missing numbers. The first one has been done for you.

Note for parent: On a separate piece of paper, ask your child to write out as sums the addition facts shown on the tin cans, using the + and = symbols they have learned.

Write the missing numbers.

🍭 + 2 = 4   🍭 + 3 = 6   4 + 🍭 = 8

5 + 🍭 = 10   🍭 + 8 = 10   6 + 🍭 = 10

🍭 + 7 = 10   1 + 🍭 = 10   🍭 + 0 = 10

Follow these trails to reach 10.
Write the missing totals.

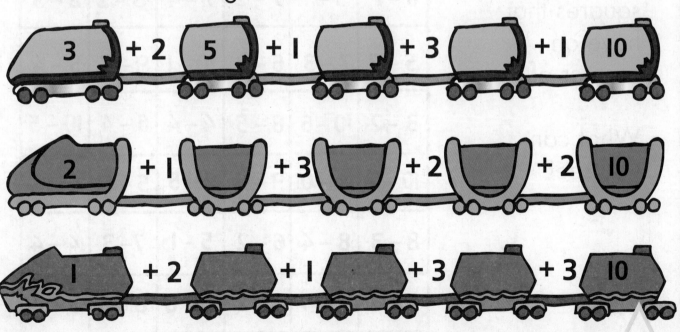

3 + 2 [5] + 1 [ ] + 3 [ ] + 1 [10]

2 + 1 [ ] + 3 [ ] + 2 [ ] + 2 [10]

1 + 2 [ ] + 1 [ ] + 3 [ ] + 3 [10]

121

Subtraction practice

Write the answers in the boxes. Use the number track to help you.

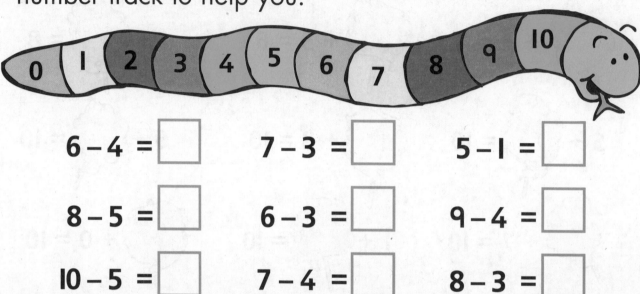

6 – 4 = ☐   7 – 3 = ☐   5 – 1 = ☐

8 – 5 = ☐   6 – 3 = ☐   9 – 4 = ☐

10 – 5 = ☐   7 – 4 = ☐   8 – 3 = ☐

Colour the squares that have an answer of 4.

What can you see?

6 – 1	5 – 1	7 – 2	7 – 4	8 – 2	8 – 3
5 – 2	7 – 3	6 – 3	10 – 1	9 – 7	5 – 4
3 – 2	10 – 6	8 – 5	4 – 4	6 – 4	10 – 5
10 – 7	4 – 0	9 – 6	9 – 5	5 – 0	6 – 5
8 – 3	8 – 4	6 – 2	5 – 1	7 – 3	4 – 4
5 – 3	9 – 4	7 – 1	10 – 6	8 – 6	3 – 0

Note for parent: On a separate piece of paper, ask your child to write out the subtractions shown in the squares and include the answers, using the – and = symbols they have learned.

Write the missing numbers.

⬡ − 5 = 5

▲ − 4 = 4

⬤ − 3 = 3

4 −  = 2

10 − ⬡ = 4

10 − ⬛ = 8

 − 3 = 7

⬟ − 8 = 2

10 − ✦ = 1

Draw a line to join each pair of stars with the same answer.

4 − 3

8 − 5

9 − 7

10 − 3

9 − 2

7 − 4

6 − 4

7 − 6

English answers

Page 8

man, red, pig, sock, jet, duck, bus, bed, log, fish, crab, men.

Page 9

dog, fox, log;
hat, bat, fan;
bell, web, peg;
sum, jug, bus;
six, pig, lips.

Page 10

Row 1: book; row 2: tree; row 3: cat; row 4: house; row 5: bicycle.

Page 11

The teacher is under the table – no; The girl is reading a book – yes; The boy is painting the door – no; The teacher is looking at the girl – yes;
The cat is reading a book – no;
The boy has got a brush – yes;
The hamster is on its cage – no.

Page 14

clock, bridge, crown, black;
green, plug, drill, flag.

Page 15

sp: spider, spoon, spanner;
st: stool, stamp, star;
sn: snail, snake, snowman;
sw: swan, switch, swing.

Page 16

cl – clown, dr – drum, sn – snail;
bl – blue, gr – grapes;
sp – spider, st – star, sw – swan.

Page 18

Everyone fell over and the turnip came out. **D**
The farmer saw an enormous turnip. **A**

Everyone tried to pull up the turnip. **C**
The farmer tried to pull up the turnip. **B**

Page 20

ball, dog, cat; b, c, d.
house, fish, girl; f, g, h.
ladybird, moon, key; k, l, m.
rabbit, queen, parachute; p, q, r.
umbrella, seesaw, television; s, t, u.

Page 21

or – fork, us – bus, an – man;
all – ball, am – lamb, in – twins;
at – bat.

Page 22

A little girl put on her dress.
The sun was hot.
I like getting into my bed to go to sleep.
I can see a bird's nest in the tree.
Dad kicked the ball.
A little boy put on his football boots.

Page 23

What is the time?
I like to eat fruit.
When do I go to school?
The car was going fast.
Who went up the hill with Jill?
The cat likes to sit on my lap.

There are 8 capital letters.

Page 24

Alison, Imran, Isabella, Jamilla, Meena, Oscar, Samuel, William.

Page 25

Wednesday, Saturday, Thursday, Friday, Sunday, Tuesday, Monday.

Page 27

9827, 9026, 9146, 9544.
Ms Walker, Mr Anderson, Mrs Todd, Mrs Depster.

Page 28

elephant: A large animal with a long trunk and ivory tusks. It lives in Africa and Asia.

kangaroo: A large animal that can jump very well. It carries its young in a pouch. It comes from Australia.

monkey: A small animal with long arms and feet that it uses like hands. It lives in jungles.

panda: A black and white animal like a bear. It lives in China.

zebra: An animal like a horse with black and white stripes. It lives in Africa.

Page 29

giraffes, penguins, whales, bears, turtles.
10, 4, 20, 18, 14.

Page 30

Things I eat: apple, banana, egg, grapes, sandwich.

Things I see on wheels: bicycle, bus, car, train, van.

Page 31

Things I use in the kitchen: food processor, frying pan, knife, pan, spoon.

Things I use in the garden: fork, lawnmower, spade, watering can, wheelbarrow.

Phonics answers

Pages 36–37

The missing letters are:
c, f, g, l, n, r, u, x, y.

Page 38

The missing letters are:
b, c, e, g, h, j, k, m.

Page 39

The missing letters are:
o, r, s, u, x, y.

Page 40

ball/wall, balloon/moon, bee/tree, nail/snail, carrot/parrot.

Page 41

flag, clown, dragon, spoon.
clock, grapes, flower, drum.

Page 42

The correct middle sounds are:
hat, sun, mop, net, pig, cup, van, fox, six.

Page 44

toothbrush, shed, telephone, fork, cup, spoon, sheet, man.

Page 45

The missing letters are: c and f.
dragon, clown, spoon.

Page 46

bat – cat, fox – box, jar – car, dog – log.

Page 47

butterfly – but, butter, fly, utter;
heart – art, ear, he, hear;
window – do, in, win, wind;
snail – ail, nail; hand – an, and;
caterpillar – at, ate, cat, cater, ill, pill, pillar.

Page 48

bridge/brick, skeleton/skier, dragon/dress, grass/grapes, clown/cloud.

Page 49

clock, slide, train, spider, twins, frog.

Page 50

fish, egg, duck – d, e, f;
igloo, horse, goat – g, h, i;
key, lemon, jellyfish – j, k, l;
nurse, orange, moon – m, n, o.

Page 51

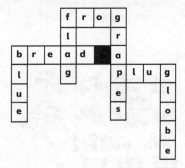

Page 52

bus, pig, bee, cup, sun, cap.

Page 53

1. ship, 2. sheep, 3. shoes,
4. shark, 5. shell, 6. shorts.

Page 54

bus, dog, bat, drum, crab, fork, cup, ten.

Page 55

Possible answers are: cherries/chocolate, train/tractor, straws/strawberries, swan/switch, drum/drawing, crocodile/crayons.

Page 56

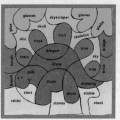

The animal is a dinosaur.

Page 57

ducks, pigs, cows, farmers, cats.

Page 58

sn: snail/snow/snake;
cr: crocodile/crayon/crab;
sp: spider/spade/spoon;
fl: fly/flower/flag.

Page 59

1. ship, 2. sheep, 3. shell.
cows, farmers, cats.

Page 60

str + ing = string;
tr + ain = train;
gl + asses = glasses;
bl + ack = black;
ch + erries = cherries;
scr + ew = screw.

Page 61

sock/duck, brush/fish, car/star, switch/witch.

Page 62

cub/cube, pip/pipe, fir/fire, cap/cape.

Page 63

transport: car/bus/train;
food: banana/bread/apple;
animals: tiger/giraffe/lion.

Maths answers

Page 68

8 spots, 10 spots, 6 spots, 9 spots, 7 spots, 4 spots.

Page 69

Clockwise from left: 10 + 0 = 10 spots, 7 + 3 = 10 spots, 9 + 1 = 10 spots, 6 + 4 = 10 spots, 5 + 5 = 10 spots, 8 + 2 = 10 spots, 4 + 6 = 10 spots.

Page 70

3 and 2 make 5 altogether, 2 and 4 make 6 altogether.
Buttons: 1 + 6 = 7; stars: 4 + 3 = 7; sweets: 5 + 2 = 7; hearts: 6 + 3 = 9.

Page 71

3 + 5 = 8, 4 + 4 = 8, 1 + 5 = 6, 2 + 5 = 7.

Page 72

Row 1: 4 take away 2 leaves 2, 6 take away 2 leaves 4, 5 take away 2 leaves 3; row 2: 8 take away 2 leaves 6, 7 take away 2 leaves 5, 10 take away 2 leaves 8; row 3: 3 − 2 = 1, 2 − 2 = 0, 9 − 2 = 7.

Page 73

Page 74

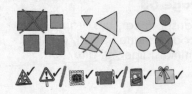

Page 75

Rectangles, triangles, circles, squares.

Page 76

Page 78

Row 1 – cubes, row 2 – cylinders, row 3 – spheres, row 4 – cuboids.

Page 79

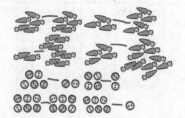

Page 80

△ triangle, ◯ circle, ▭ rectangle, ☐ square.

Page 81

Red bags = ✗; yellow bags = ✔.

Page 82

1 + 4 = 5, 3 + 3 = 6, 4 + 6 = 10.
4 + 6 = 10, 8 + 2 = 10.

Page 83

4 + 3 = 7, 2 + 5 = 7, 6 + 2 = 8, 3 + 3 = 6, 6 + 3 = 9, 1 + 5 = 6.
Total of 4: red and yellow scarves; total of 6: orange and dark-blue scarves; total of 7: pink and bright-blue scarves; total of 10: green and purple scarves.

Page 84

4 − 2 = 2, 7 − 3 = 4, 8 − 5 = 3, 5 − 2 = 3, 7 − 4 = 3.

Page 85

4 − 1 = 3, 5 − 3 = 2, 8 − 7 = 1, 5 − 5 = 0, 9 − 5 = 4, 10 − 2 = 8.
10 − 5 and 5 − 0; 8 − 7 and 6 − 5; 10 − 7 and 6 − 3.

Page 86

11 o'clock, 8 o'clock, 5 o'clock.

Page 87

From left to right: half-past 4, half-past 10, half-past 7.

Page 88

Page 89

2 + 4 = 6, 3 + 3 = 6, 5 + 4 = 9, 6 + 4 = 10, 5 + 5 = 10, 2 + 3 = 5, 1 + 7 = 8, 2 + 7 = 9, 2 + 2 = 4.
10 − 1 = 9, 5 − 3 = 2, 4 − 2 = 2, 8 − 3 = 5, 7 − 4 = 3, 6 − 5 = 1, 10 − 6 = 4, 9 − 6 = 3, 7 − 2 = 5.

Page 90

Top train: 9, 10, 11, 12, 13, 14, 15, 16, 17. Middle train: 11, 12, 13, 14, 15, 16, 17, 18, 19, 20. Bottom train: 7, 8, 9, 10, 11, 12, 13, 14, 15, 16.
Eleven – 11, fourteen – 14, twelve – 12, fifteen – 15, twenty – 20, sixteen – 16, thirteen – 13, seventeen – 17.

Page 91

Clockwise from top left: rhinoceros, tiger, monkey, elephant.

Page 92

8 + 3 = 11, 9 + 5 = 14, 8 + 7 = 15, 6 + 7 = 13, 9 + 9 = 18, 6 + 4 = 10.
10 + 3 = 13, 10 + 5 = 15, 10 + 8 = 18, 12 + 6 = 18, 10 + 10 = 20, 15 + 1 = 16.

Page 93

12 − 8 = 4, 12 − 6 = 6, 13 − 4 = 9, 11 − 9 = 2, 16 − 8 = 8, 12 − 5 = 7.
20 − 4 = 16, 20 − 5 = 15, 20 − 6 = 14, 20 − 8 = 12, 20 − 2 = 18, 20 − 7 = 13.

Adding and taking away answers

Pages 96–97
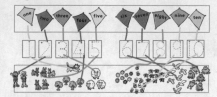

Page 98

Page 99
There should be more spaceships coloured red than blue in each box. 9 spaceships altogether, 10 spaceships altogether.

Pages 100–101
6 biscuits altogether, 6 cakes altogether, 5 pizzas altogether, 7 ice creams altogether, 9 sweets altogether. 3 and 2 make 5 altogether, 4 and 3 make 7 altogether, 6 and 2 make 8 altogether.

Page 102
5 take away 2 leaves 3, 6 take away 2 leaves 4, 8 take away 2 leaves 6, 4 take away 2 leaves 2, 9 take away 3 leaves 6.

Page 103
5 children, 4 chairs, difference = 1. 7 children, 5 chairs, difference = 2. 6 children, 3 chairs, difference = 3.

Pages 104–105
4 sweets add 2 sweets = 6 sweets, 6 sweets add 1 sweet = 7 sweets, 5 sweets add 3 sweets = 8 sweets, 7 sweets add 2 sweets = 9 sweets. 6 drinks take away 1 drink = 5 drinks, 5 drinks take away 3 drinks = 2 drinks, 3 drinks take away 2 drinks = 1 drink, 7 drinks take away 4 drinks = 3 drinks.

Page 106
6 biscuits altogether, 6 cakes altogether. 6 and 2 make 8 altogether. 8 take away 2 leaves 6, 4 take away 2 leaves 2.

Page 107

eleven	11
twelve	12
thirteen	13
fourteen	14
fifteen	15
sixteen	16
seventeen	17
eighteen	18
nineteen	19
twenty	20

Pages 108–109
2 + 3 = 5, 3 + 4 = 7, 4 + 5 = 9. 3 + 5 = 8 altogether, 4 + 2 = 6 altogether. 3 + 2 = 5, 2 + 2 = 4, 4 + 3 = 7, 5 + 1 = 6, 6 + 3 = 9, 4 + 5 = 9.

Pages 110–111
7 − 2 = 5, 5 − 2 = 3, 8 − 2 = 6. Parents need to check child's answer for the last sum on page 18. 5 balls take away 3 balls = 2 balls, 4 balls take away 2 balls = 2 balls, 8 balls take away 4 balls = 4 balls.

Pages 112–113
4 + 2 = 6, 5 + 4 = 9, 7 + 3 = 10, 11 + 2 = 13, 14 + 5 = 19, 13 + 7 = 20. 5 + 2 = 7, 4 + 1 = 5, 3 + 3 = 6, 6 + 3 = 9, 3 + 1 = 4. The missing numbers are: blue rocket – 6, 9, 10; green rocket – 1, 3, 4, 8; red rocket – 8, 9, 12, 15.

Pages 114–115
6 − 3 = 3, 5 − 2 = 3, 8 − 4 = 4, 13 − 1 = 12, 16 − 3 = 13, 17 − 6 = 11.

Pages 116–117
2: 0 + 2, 1 + 1, 2 + 0. 3: 1 + 2, 2 + 1, 3 + 0. 4: 1 + 3, 2 + 2, 3 + 1. 5: 1 + 4, 2 + 3, 3 + 2.

A rabbit and a carrot are hidden among the shapes.

Page 118
1: 2 − 1, 3 − 2, 4 − 3, 5 − 4, 10 − 9. 2: 5 − 3, 4 − 2, 3 − 1, 2 − 0, 10 − 8. Possible answers include: 6 − 1, 7 − 2, 8 − 3, 9 − 4

Page 119
5 + 2 = 7, 4 + 1 = 5, 4 + 4 = 8. 5 balls take away 3 balls = 2 balls, 4 balls take away 3 balls = 1 ball.

Pages 120–121
4 + 3 = 7, 6 + 2 = 8, 5 + 5 = 10, 9 + 1 = 10, 7 + 2 = 9, 3 + 5 = 8, 2 + 4 = 6, 4 + 4 = 8, 6 + 3 = 9. Missing numbers: row 1: 6, 8; row 2: 10, 9, 8, 10. 2 + 2 = 4, 3 + 3 = 6, 4 + 4 = 8, 5 + 5 = 10, 2 + 8 = 10, 6 + 4 = 10, 3 + 7 = 10, 1 + 9 = 10, 10 + 0 = 10. Missing totals: green train: 6, 9; purple train: 3, 6, 8; red train: 3, 4, 7.

Pages 122–123
6 − 4 = 2, 7 − 3 = 4, 5 − 1 = 4, 8 − 5 = 3, 6 − 3 = 3, 9 − 4 = 5, 10 − 5 = 5, 7 − 4 = 3, 8 − 3 = 5.

The number 4 is hidden in the grid.

10 − 5 = 5, 8 − 4 = 4, 6 − 3 = 3, 4 − 2 = 2, 10 − 6 = 4, 10 − 2 = 8, 10 − 3 = 7, 10 − 8 = 2, 10 − 9 = 1.